JIMMY GREAVES

JIMMY GREAVES

FourFourTwo | *great footballers*

Matt Allen

Published in Great Britain in 2001 by
Virgin Publishing Ltd
Thames Wharf Studios
Rainville Road
London W6 9HA

A catalogue record for the book is available
from the British Library.

ISBN 1 85227 956 7

Typeset by TW Typesetting, Plymouth, Devon

Printed and bound in Great Britain by
Creative Print and Design (Wales), Ebbw Vale

Contents

Acknowledgements

Firstly, an apology.

I've never seen Jimmy Greaves play for Spurs.

Sure, I've seen the video clips and the re-runs of his great goals on TV. I've had his impressive goal ratio thrown at me every other Saturday when I meet with older friends in N17 and we discuss the merits of Lineker, Klinsmann, Rebrov and Allen. I know he scored 220 goals in a Spurs shirt between the years of 1961 and 1970. And I know he was one of the quickest predators ever to have stalked the penalty areas of White Hart Lane. But unfortunately, I'm too young ever to have seen his talents at first hand, so I'd like to thank the following people for giving me an insight into the real Jimmy Greaves.

Without the help of Cliff Jones and Alan Mullery, I wouldn't have been able to get the first-hand recollections of Greavsie's Spurs career. I'd also like to thank the Spurs press office for patiently helping me with my persistent queries. Hopefully, the Glory years will come back soon. And cheer up Cliff, we're not that bad these days.

In addition to those involved with Tottenham, I would like to thank the following: Barry Fry, Les Eason and Andrew Sleight for the Barnet story, and Brian Mears and Ian Macleay for their help with Greavsie's Chelsea days and contacts.

I'd also like to acknowledge the help of Bob and Dan Abrahams, both of whom tied up the loose ends; those at West Ham for their help and encouragement; Barnet FC; the AC Milan press office; the FA; Chelsea FC; and

Olivia Blair for the phone numbers. The list at the back names all the books that have been so vital to my research, so thanks to all the authors mentioned for their assistance – especially Greavsie and Bill Nicholson.

And of course, the book wouldn't have got anywhere without the help of those at *FourFourTwo*. So cheers to the following: Leo Moynihan, Pilfer, Michael Hann, Stig, Louis Massarella, Ewan Buck, Steve 'Mondial' Bidmead, Justin Barnes, Richard Pendleton, Tim Barnett, Paul Simpson, Cormac Bourne, Mike Skyte, Owen Norris (come on you Spurs!), Rachel Sullivan and all the work experience kids for the photocopying and tape transcribing. It was a boring job, I know, but it's better than making the tea.

Beers and encouragement were also provided by a number of people, especially when Jimmy Greaves turned into 'Jimmy Grief' in the closing months: Nick Caley, Anna Erlandsson, Lou Cannon (I told you so), Richard Knott, Georgina Bowman, Wendy Stone, Katherine Green, Richard Lonsdale, Aaron Brown, Judith Addleson and Bungle. I told you I'd finish it! Plus Doves, Slint, Badly Drawn Boy and Guided By Voices for the inspiration. Ta.

Finally, I'd like to thank Mum, Dad, Katie and Joanna for nagging me when shelf stacking seemed like a good way to earn a living. It was you who pushed me here, so if the rest of you have any problems with the book, you know who's responsible.

With a combination of the information and help provided by the people above and a lot of back-breaking research, this book should go some way to providing the definitive story of one of England's greatest players. I hope it's as enjoyable to read as it was to write.

Cheers.

Matt Allen
December 2000

Introduction

Jimmy Greaves of Chelsea is one British inside forward I think worthy of a place among the truly great footballers of the moment. There have been many reasons put forward for Jimmy Greaves' success as possibly the greatest goalscorer in present-day football, and, as an opponent, I believe everything stems from Jimmy's ability to take his time. Greaves, no matter what the situation in which he finds himself, never gets excited. The calm a truly great player must possess never leaves him.

DAVE MACKAY, 1962

Fifteen years ago, former Spurs manager Bill Nicholson advanced the argument that were Jimmy Greaves playing today he would be worth far more than any professional footballer in the world. It's an interesting thought, and it raises an important point: to what degree would a player of Jimmy Greaves' calibre be valued in the modern game? In a league based on financial gain, how much would a Premiership club pay for a player blessed with Greaves' skill and footballing intelligence? Ten million? Twenty million? Thirty million, even? Certainly the twenty-first-century football club seems determined without a second look to brandish large cheques under the noses of unproven European strikers and players who have banged in a fair number of goals for struggling First Division sides. So how much would a Manchester United, Leeds or Liverpool be prepared to pay for someone of Greaves' undoubted talents if he were playing top-flight football today?

It makes you wonder. Last season alone, Manchester United were prepared to secure the services of Ruud van Nistelrooy in a transfer worth £18 million. The deal fell through on a medical technicality, but the episode nonetheless serves to highlight the value of the modern player – and this a youthful player with exciting potential, still a long way off from being the finished article. Sure, van Nistelrooy had a few international caps under his belt and was scoring a phenomenal amount of goals in the Dutch First Division, but is that really enough to justify breaking the English transfer record? Eighteen million pounds for a striker who has done nothing more than score an impressive tally of goals in a league that traditionally acts as a breeding ground for young talent? Albeit competitive, is the Premier League just a cosy place for internationals to pick up a comfortable pay cheque, or is the splashing out of cash on overseas forwards indicative of the lack of quality in the English striker?

And what of Chelsea's £10 million cheque for Chris Sutton, before his eventual move to Celtic in 2000? If a player who had only scored a handful in his last season with Blackburn Rovers and notched up the average defender's goal tally in his first season at the club was worth £10 million, what price Jimmy Greaves in the twenty-first century? Greaves was arguably the greatest goalscorer in English football, hitting the net 357 times in 516 appearances in the old First Division for Chelsea, Spurs and West Ham and 44 times in 57 full England appearances – an international goalscoring record that has only been bettered by Bobby Charlton and Gary Lineker, both with considerably more performances in an England shirt. What's more, Greaves was one of English football's first European exports; despite having an unhappy time during his three-month spell in Milan, he still managed to score nine goals in fourteen appearances in a country known for stifling attacking football.

When we think of the modern goalscoring greats in English football, none of them has the all-round ability, flair and vision of Jimmy Greaves. Alan Shearer has a tremendous physical presence in the box and an ability to turn defenders with his strength; Michael Owen has a turn of pace that can leave his marker standing flat-footed, and a deadly eye for goal that was so wonderfully highlighted during the 1998 World Cup second-round defeat at the hands of Argentina; while Kevin Phillips has the anticipation and instinct that saw him claim the Adidas/*FourFourTwo* Golden Boot in his first season in the Premiership, silencing Sunderland's critics at the same time. But despite the obvious talents of our top strikers, none of these players seems to possess every goalscoring attribute in their armoury.

The only player who comes close to owning the complete package in goalscoring terms is Robbie Fowler, a player blessed with speed, strength, anticipation, aerial power and the skill and dexterity to walk the ball around a posse of defenders, past the goalkeeper and into an empty net. Sadly, injury has hindered Fowler's performances in recent seasons, but that hasn't stopped figures in excess of £12 million being bandied around in the press during the close season's inevitable transfer rumour mill.

As a goalscorer, Jimmy Greaves had it all. Sadly, to most people under the age of 40 he is little more than a red-top tabloid column writer, the dry sidekick of the ever-giggling Ian St John on ITV's Saturday lunchtime show *Saint and Greavsie*, or the caricature on the satirical TV show *Spitting Image*. However, those fortunate enough to have witnessed Greaves at his peak will know there has been a lot more to his career than stinging references to the ineptitude of Scottish goalkeepers and the scathing criticism of England managers.

Blessed with speed, skill and an anticipation that seemed to give him a five-yard head start over most defenders, Greaves was a joy to watch at his peak – a peak that materialised during his eight seasons with Spurs, as he quickly became a crowd-pleaser who still ranks alongside flair players such as Danny Blanch-flower, Glenn Hoddle, Paul Gascoigne and David Ginola, so beloved by the Tottenham faithful. He was a creative entertainer who generated a ripple of excitement around the ground whenever he took the ball at his feet or side-stepped a defender's challenge. It was a talent warmly received by both fans and managers alike as Greaves destroyed the most resolute of defences.

'I wanted him the moment he scored his first goal in League football on his Chelsea debut at White Hart Lane,' recalled Spurs manager Bill Nicholson, the man who signed Greaves for a then record-breaking £99,999 from Italian club AC Milan in 1961.

I will never forget it. What a tremendous goal it was. He beat three defenders before stroking the ball into the net. It had the hallmarks of his game: improvisation and genius.

Greaves had the natural gift of timing. When confronted by the goalkeeper he seemed to be able to whip the ball into the net almost every time, while other forwards in a similar position would often find the keeper making a fine save. Greaves gave the keeper no chance. He rarely blasted the ball, though I did see him score a twenty-yarder against Burnley which hit the back of the net at a very high speed.

Sometimes the ball would come towards him and you thought the defender who was marking him would get it before he did, but he would stick out a foot and knock it away. Even when he was late, he seemed capable of winning a rebound off his shins and the ball would fall conveniently for him to shoot. His ratio of success was unmatched.

After joining Spurs following the club's record-breaking League and FA Cup Double season in 1960/61, Greaves would have been forgiven for slipping into the shadows of one of England's greatest ever club sides and struggling to shine in a squad full of experienced stars such as Danny Blanchflower, John White and Dave Mackay. Instead, he became the jewel in Bill Nicholson's crown, scoring 30 goals in his first season at White Hart Lane. Greaves immediately became a crowd favourite and the scourge of defenders throughout the English First Division.

In eight seasons he notched up 220 goals in a Spurs shirt, leading the First Division goalscoring charts four times, as well as carrying on the record of scoring on his debut for every team he played for. He became the striker players loved to team up with, both at club and international level – an anticipator of passes, a master of flick-ons and crosses, all done with an almost telepathic certainty. In turn, he was the one player defenders would dread seeing pinned up on the team sheet.

Greaves' reputation was such that Spurs wing-half Dave Mackay was singing his praises before the striker even made his move from AC Milan to Spurs at the end of 1961.

Greaves, so light on his feet and quick in his thinking, never allows anything to upset his poise. If he fails to take advantage of an opening he has created for himself, or has been created for him, he never appears to lose heart or confidence. Disappointment seems to act as a spur, and this, coupled with his obvious love of the game, has made him a forward no defence can ever allow an inch in which to work.

Jimmy, like all outstanding players, takes up positions which in themselves worry a defence. He creates his own open spaces, and my answer to those who say he is a 'lucky' player – some have even called Jimmy a 'poacher' – are talking out of the back of their necks. Greaves gets goals because he is always in the right place at the right time. He never loses his poise, and when he shoots Jimmy does not make a half-hearted effort. It's a full-blooded drive – the effort of a man who has confidence in his ability.

A former England striker and scorer of that hat-trick against Germany in the 1966 World Cup final, Geoff Hurst was equally complimentary about Greaves' talents.

> Greaves was a mate. I had always held him in awe since I got to know him when he trained with us at West Ham just before he moved to Milan. I was impressed by his icy professionalism. Jim is a great kidder. Off the park he laughs it up a lot and appears to take nothing seriously, especially football. It's a false front . . . he is one of the most calculating pros I know. Just watch him when there's a chance of a goal around. He tingles with alertness. He never goes for the 'flash' shot, the fancy move: he only beats opponents when he has to . . . then it's a quick shot directed with a surgeon's skill into the place the goalkeeper will find hardest to cover.

'He had blistering pace up front,' recalled former Spurs team-mate Alan Mullery.

> People talk about Michael Owen's pace, but he's got nothing compared to Greavsie. Over fifteen to twenty yards no one could touch him. He was too quick. I think he must have given defenders nightmares. His first touch was incredible and he was equally good with both feet. He was just an outstanding player all round, and of course he had this incredible knack of scoring goals. No defences or defenders could hold him and he was a 30-goal-a-season player every year. It was wonderful to watch. He could score wherever he played. Chelsea. Milan. Spurs. Wherever.
> As a character at the club, Greavsie was great. But there was a stack of characters at the club in those days. He was a lovely bloke and a terrible joker. I don't think he could resist it. He would never stop. He used to smoke a pipe in those days. He looked like Sherlock Holmes. But his easy-going attitude was

as important to the Spurs as his goals. He was always good at easing the nerves. He would never get agitated, even before a cup final [Mullery and Greaves played together in the 1967 FA Cup final]. He was always as calm as you like. He would be joking in the dressing room and geeing everybody up. He knew he had a fabulous talent and he would just get on with it. He had faith in his own ability.

It's players like Greaves that make the game. Crowd-pleasers, entertainers, mavericks, call them what you like – they're footballers with the ability to turn a game in an instant, to bring the crowd to their feet to strain over the tops of heads in order to snatch that brief glimpse of something special, something different, that makes the game the great spectacle it is. Ask any Manchester United fan why he queues for his ticket three weeks before a game and he won't talk about a desire to watch the Neville brothers put in another assured defensive display along the flanks, or Jaap Stam command his back four's offside trap. He'll wax lyrical about David Beckham's pinpoint crosses to the feet of grateful strikers, Ryan Giggs' hypnotising dribbles, Roy Keane's no-nonsense control in midfield, the audacity of Dwight Yorke and Andy Cole.

The game is about entertainers, not stiflers. We want to see the Maradonas, Cruyffs and Rivaldos of the football world embarrass opponents with their skill and confidence. We pay to see Paolo Di Canio scissor-volley a ball past a stranded goalkeeper, Harry Kewell side-foot an arcing chip over the head of the keeper and into the back of the net, Thierry Henry steamroller his way down the Arsenal wing. For most of us the dour headless-chicken style of Wimbledon's zonal marking or a George Graham back four storming twenty yards forward with their arms raised in triumph as they catch another hapless striker offside is a frustrating anticlimax.

In the 1960s fans paid to see Tottenham Hotspur because they were entertainers, on their day the most exciting team in Europe, a side capable of demolishing the opposition not only with intelligent, pacy football but with flair and, on occasion, arrogance. On winning the Double at Wembley in 1961, a despondent Bill Nicholson claimed the game was a disappointment, his side winning the FA Cup in a disciplined and unentertaining fashion. It was the greatest moment in the club's history, yet the lack of flair bothered him. Grinding out results wasn't what his Tottenham team were all about. In an echo of Nicholson's passion for exciting football, Danny Blanchflower was famously to remark later that 'The game's about glory. It's about doing things in style, with a flourish. It's about going out and beating the other lot, not waiting for them to die of boredom.'

Greaves had that style and flourish. His technical ability could almost have been based on the Tottenham way. It was no surprise that the Tottenham crowd took to his intelligent play. He loved the football, keeping it at his feet whenever he ran; dropping a shoulder to confuse an oncoming defender; sweeping the ball away from a marker's boot; rolling his studs over it before pushing it through the oncoming keeper's legs; running around him to pick it up on the other side and clip it into an empty goal. Greaves had the style to slip into Bill Nicholson's Glory side as if he had been groomed for a career at Tottenham. But more importantly, he had the ability to score goals seemingly at will, helping Spurs secure the FA Cup in his first season as well as a European Cup Winners' Cup in 1963 and another FA Cup in 1967. It was the most successful decade in Tottenham Hotspur's history, with Jimmy Greaves spearheading the attack.

Of course as a sportsman he wasn't going to be without his flaws. Former England manager Walter Winterbottom once claimed that 'Tottenham were the best exponents of push and run, which suited Danny's [Blanchflower] skills and his intelligence. He would always look for the ball, offering himself to whoever was in possession. I used to get cross with Jimmy Greaves because he'd sometimes hide if things weren't going well, which was wrong. No one could use the ball better than Jimmy when he had it and so I always wanted him to show himself to pick up possession.'

Training never came easy to him; he often preferred to play in goal than out on the pitch. It would infuriate his team-mates and managers alike to see him fooling around during the week, only for their frustration to turn to gratitude when he would invariably turn the game with a quickness of foot or a deft finish that would secure two points or salvage a draw from a game Tottenham seemed destined to lose. Joe Kinnear has fond memories of Greaves' lethargic attitude to training, recalling how the striker would often hitch a lift back to the training ground during pre-season long-distance runs.

Jimmy Greaves never had to work at his game. He was just so talented. In training all he mainly did was practise goalscoring. It was amazing to watch him. Apart from that, he didn't like training and hated stuff like running or cross-country. When we had to do it he would beg lifts on milk floats, or hide a bike and ride it home. If he was forced to do the whole run, because Eddie Bailey or somebody was watching his every step, he'd come in half an hour after most of us had gone home. If he still hadn't appeared, one of the lads would go and pick him up in his car.

'There were areas of Greaves' game where he had deficiencies,' Bill Nicholson recalled.

He wasn't a tackler and didn't much like having to chase or harass defenders. Nor was he good in the air. He did not like training but, like so many geniuses, he realised that his gift had to be worked at and he would practise scoring like a golfer practises his swing. Sometimes the other players would complain he hadn't worked hard enough in a game. 'But he's in the team for his goals,' I would reply. 'Who scored the goals last week? Goalscoring is something you can't all do, but he can do it better than anyone.' Often Alan Gilzean would say at half-time: 'We're going to get nothing out of this game.' And in the 89th minute, Jimmy Greaves would pop up and score the winner.

Sadly, like all geniuses, Greaves' character was flawed. During the bad times in his career he would often turn to drink as a psychological crutch, spending his spare time in pubs and clubs with friends and then, as time went on and he slipped into alcoholism, alone. Unfortunately there were several times in his career when life seemed impossible without the assistance of a drinking binge. It was the death of his first son, Jimmy Junior, and a disastrous move abroad to AC Milan in 1961 that first pushed Greaves into a corner, forcing him to turn to the bottle in order to escape the nightmare of a lonely life a long way from home. The move to Spurs briefly pulled him out of this slump, but further disappointments in the shape of his absence from the World Cup-winning team in 1966 following the emergence of Geoff Hurst in the latter stages of the tournament, and his transfer from Spurs to a disappointing West Ham side in 1970, quickly set Greaves back.

The drinking soon began to affect his life and those around him, eventually leading to the break-up of his marriage with Irene and his subsequent divorce from top-flight football in 1971. Ironically, it was the love of his team-mates and football that had first introduced him to alcohol, in the post-match pub sessions that would invariably follow a Saturday afternoon game. Greaves was a sociable character and loved nothing more than to mix with his colleagues after a game to conduct a post-mortem on the afternoon's performance, no matter how well or badly they had played. It was only when his career took bad turns that he drank to excess.

To ignore his alcoholism would only serve to ignore certain elements of Greaves' character and ambition – why else would a player despair at being dropped from a World Cup final team if he wasn't of an ambitious nature? Why else would a player turn to drink as he saw the best years of his football career fading if he didn't have the desire to compete at the highest level for as long as possible? Ambition drove Greaves throughout his career. The frustration of not seeing his ambitions realised nearly crippled him.

But to dwell on Greaves' shortcomings would only overshadow the achievements of one of the game's most remarkable players. If we can forget the critical columns in the *Sun* and the dramatic tabloid headlines that highlighted the fall from grace during his lowest ebb, we can see Jimmy Greaves for the exciting, gifted player he was, and the reformed character he has become. Now, Greaves can see the pain he caused to himself and those around him during those drinking binges. It took a courageous and public battle against the booze before the player could rebuild his life as a TV pundit. Only now can he look back on those days without wincing, as anyone who has sat through one of his humorous after-dinner speeches can testify.

'I suppose the start of my drink problem probably happened in Italy when I joined AC Milan in 1961,' he said during a recent speech.

Gazza was at Lazio, but it was a different world when I was in Italy. There are ten flights to Milan each day now, yet when I was out there, there were only two flights to Italy a week! And I was usually so pissed I missed them both. We had a trainer called Rocco who had to be seen to be believed. He was about six foot eight and he had connections with some really weird people. He would put a note on my door telling me the 'do's and don'ts', and if I took no notice I would find a horse's head in my bed. Sometimes people would say I was drunk when I didn't know I was drunk. The leaning Tower of Pisa looked all right to me.

I've had controversy wherever I've been. Dropped for the World Cup final in 1966, AC Milan, drink problems, the lot . . . If I was George Best it might be a different story. The thing about George is he's still on the bottle now and I'm not. I've cleaned up my act and I don't touch the stuff now. But what really pisses me off is that George looks better for it! Look at me, and look at him. I got most of my habits off him in the 1960s. His speciality was whisky and Windolene. He'd say to me, 'It's the perfect combination, Jim. You still wake up pissed but your eyes are clear as a bell.' He's still a cult hero in Ireland even now. They asked him to launch a ship, but it took them three hours to get the bottle out of his hands. We were approached by a publishing company to write about our times in the 1960s, but we couldn't remember a single thing about it. So if any of you out there know where the hell we were in the 1960s, could you drop us a line?

Greaves may not be able to remember the effect he had on a Tottenham team in the Glory years, but those of us familiar with White Hart Lane will have one enduring image of the player. A brief, grainy clip of film of the great side of the 1960s is shown on the huge TV screens at either end of the ground before every game. Among the collection of great moments in Spurs history, and alongside Ricky Villa's mesmerising goal against Manchester City in the 1981 FA Cup final and the UEFA Cup triumph of 1984, stands a brief reminder of Jimmy Greaves' talent. Picking the ball up inside the opposition's half, Greaves weaves his way past four defenders and a helpless goalkeeper before slipping the ball into the net and wheeling away in delight. It's a breathtaking piece of footage that does as much to underline the superiority of Bill Nicholson's Tottenham side as it does to highlight the genius of Jimmy Greaves in his pomp.

Looking up at the huge screens at White Hart Lane and watching Greaves calmly sliding the ball into the net, it is genuinely hard to imagine how much the club would have to pay to secure a player of that sort of ability these days. Certainly very few players under the £30 million mark in European football come close to matching the grace and genius of Jimmy Greaves.

This is his story.

1 East End Boy, East End Goals

Jim was still in his U15 side, but what an awesome player even then. When the ball arrived at his feet, he would come alive, dancing around four or five players and scoring fantastic goals.

TERRY VENABLES, 1994

Dagenham is an area that seems to spawn more footballers than most areas of London. Maybe that's something to do with its sprawling estates or the quiet back streets and small scraps of wasteland and parks that encourage kids to kick a ball around whenever possible. Whatever the reason, the Docklands area situated outside the capital's famous East End has certainly produced its fair share of England's footballing peerage. In fact, during the 1950s a large crop of England's footballing family tree sprang from the area.

Terry Venables, the Chelsea and Spurs player who was later to take over as manager of Spurs, Barcelona and then England, honed his skills in the back streets of Bonham Road, while Les Allen, who played a pivotal role in the record-breaking Tottenham Double-winning side of 1961 also grew up in the area, along with his brother Dennis, who went on to play for Charlton and Reading. England World Cup-winning captain and West Ham stalwart Bobby Moore was another of Dagenham's favourite sons, as was his manager at international level, Sir Alf Ramsey.

Why Dagenham has produced so many talented footballers remains a mystery, but in the 1940s and 1950s, the area was awash with children playing football in the streets, parks or any available scrap of land that could accommodate twelve boys, a few makeshift goalposts and a concrete-worn football. Certainly there was little else for the boys to do. Dagenham at the time was a drab urban sprawl used as a relocation housing estate for families that had suffered the pain of having their houses destroyed by the Luftwaffe in the Blitz. Thousands of families were rehoused with the promise of jobs at the new Ford car factories, given the opportunity to rebuild their lives during and after the hardships of the war. For many it was the offer of a fresh start that made Dagenham so appealing, and for the kids of the area football was the only escape from a life indoors.

The area was pretty uninspiring for its inhabitants, the roads made up of long lines of red-bricked terrace houses, each one accommodating a family attracted to the estates by the promise of work and an escape from the bleak lifestyle that dominated the 1930s and 1940s. Every evening, groups of boys would be out in the street kicking a ball around the pavements, or in Valence Park, booting a ball between the ten tall trees that made for ideal goalposts, or in front of the bandstand in the middle of the park. For many of the boys in the area, the park was the nearest they got to escaping the urban sprawl of London.

Football became an obsession for the majority of youngsters. As happened in most cities, back streets were transformed into White Hart Lane or Stamford Bridge with the boys attempting to recreate the tricks of Stanley Matthews and Tom Finney. For many, the days naturally developed their own entertaining routine based around whoever owned a football. The journey to school would begin with a long walk to the gates, kicking a tennis ball around the streets. After the day's learning, the next stop would be Valence Park for the obligatory kick-around before it got too dark and homework had to be done. Jumpers and school satchels would be thrown to the floor, a scrappy pitch set out and a game involving upwards of 30 players would take place, each boy showing as much dedication and passion as a committed professional. The evening might be rounded off with a quick visit to Weston's fish and chip shop on Clifford's Corner, all the while discussing the evening's performance, the next school game or how they were going to get to the West Ham match the following Saturday.

Football in the streets was as safe as in the park. Despite the presence of the Ford motor car factory, the standards of living in Dagenham were low and very few people could afford to run a car of their own. Most of the time the streets were empty, save for the occasional patrolling police car or a wedding or funeral procession. The only hazard for a street footballer was the odd broken slab of concrete or the cast-iron pillar boxes along the side streets that could cause a nasty injury if someone was unfortunate enough to make contact with one on a blind-side run. Still, that didn't discourage the local talent from playing out there every night, much to the concern of those parents who felt their sons were paying more attention to football than they were to their studies.

Despite the hardships and the less than ideal standard of living, the people of Dagenham were happy. Jimmy Greaves certainly was. Born on 20 February 1940 in East Ham, James Peter Greaves' family moved to Dagenham when he was only six months old. The Greaves family, like thousands of others packing up and shipping out of the East End of London, was looking for an escape from the poverty and desolation of London's bomb-ravaged estates. Essex seemed the perfect choice.

Greaves' father was an underground train driver who made a comfortable living for the family. Life wasn't easy for the Greaveses, especially as the country was still coming to terms with the effects of war, but their income allowed them to have a relatively worry-free existence, and although they couldn't afford the luxuries in life, their modest wage meant they were able to provide the best for their children.

Certainly sports goods were considered a luxury, and they were rare during the 1940s as factories and companies turned their attentions to helping the war effort, but Mr Greaves, who was also the secretary of Fanshaw Old Boys club, the local football team, managed to acquire a football that had become worn and was only used for the team's kick-arounds and practice sessions. The ball wasn't in good shape, but for Greaves senior that didn't matter. It meant he could give his five-year-old son Jimmy his first taste of football.

The ball was something young Greaves took to immediately, kicking it around with his father whenever he could, but it was only later that he realised the importance of having his own ball. Following the poverty of the war, very few boys could afford a proper ball, preferring to use a bundle of rags or a worn tennis ball to play the game. Certainly these makeshift balls, being of a much smaller size and requiring a great deal more dexterity to control properly, helped the boys to improve their skills, but there was nothing like the feel of a real football. If you wanted to play like Stanley Matthews you had to have a proper football, like Stanley Matthews.

So with his proper size five football, Jimmy became the most popular kid in the street. After a day at school, the Greaves family would have to field a series of knocks at their door from boys asking if 'Jimmy was coming out to play'. More often than not they were happy to allow their son out after school, but sometimes they would become a little concerned. The fact that Jimmy was one of very few boys to have a football meant that everyone wanted to play with him, even boys who were six or seven years older than their son, who was still at primary school; most of his footballing friends were of secondary-school age. Still, that didn't bother the youngster, who relished the opportunity to mix it with lads twice his age and three times his size.

I used to play with boys a lot older. I had the ball. It was more or less a case of no Greaves, no ball. We kicked the ball so much that we'd finish up playing with the bladder. We played every day until it got dark, then we'd play around a lamppost.

I think it was those street games that taught me to evade tackles. If you remember, kids just after the war wore big black boots that weighed a ton and were built to last. If you got one of those in the shins you really knew it. I was only a titch and quickly learnt the art of nipping past an opponent. You had to be nippy or brave. I preferred to be nippy!

Not only did Jimmy's older opponents help him to develop his dribbling skills as he attempted to evade their much stronger challenges, they also helped him to compete physically. He soon learnt how to ride challenges, muscle players off the ball and tackle hard. His opponents may have been fairly gentle with him considering his smaller size (and they knew one over-physical tackle might dissuade the boy from bringing out his football next time), but it still provided a stern test of strength. Compared to his games out on the streets, football matches with players his own size and age seemed easy.

In the meantime, young Jimmy watched his first game on the terraces of Upton Park, as West Ham struggled to compete in the Second Division. Despite these experiences, his chosen club was Spurs. Jimmy loved to watch Arthur Rowe's famous 'push and run' side – a tactic that involved playing or 'pushing' the ball on to a team-mate before running into space to pick up the return pass. It was a strategy that would later earn Spurs the League championship in 1951, and it appealed to Jimmy to such an extent that he would often hunt out autographs from the Spurs players, among whose impressive first eleven were Alf Ramsey, Bill Nicholson and Eddie Bailey.

Despite the boy's obvious interest in and talent for the game, Mr Greaves never pushed his son into playing or practising, preferring to allow things to develop naturally. Indeed, it is probably down to the fact that he wasn't pushed into it that Greaves developed such a love for the game. He wouldn't have needed any encouragement anyway, but Greaves senior preferred his son to play football because he wanted to, not because he felt he had to. In fact, he couldn't scale the heights of passion his son had for the game. Sure, he had been a pretty good footballer in his time, playing as a centre-half or wing-half for a succession of amateur clubs, but he never really played the game at a higher level and had no extensive knowledge of tactics or coaching. In fact, there was absolutely no history of football in the Greaves family. Having served with the Army in India, Mr Greaves' main sport was hockey – a pastime that couldn't be catered for in the back streets of Dagenham. Nevertheless, he took an interest in his son's definite leanings towards the game, taking him out for a kick-around when his friends weren't around and giving him advice to the best of his ability whenever he needed it.

Greaves, like many great players, was self-taught. Kicking a ball around, dribbling through lampposts, dragging the ball away from the cracks in the pavement and repeatedly banging a ball against a wall was his only education, and he would spend hours practising at it, but because of his rapid development he soon found himself becoming increasingly frustrated at the lack of competitive football in the area. There were very few amateur teams in Dagenham and the East End in the late 1940s, and even the ones that did exist couldn't cater for a boy of nine years old. What's more, the Greaves family were constantly moving around Essex and east London, although their son finally settled at Smithwood Lane school in Dagenham. It was a move that pleased the youngster. Smithwood Lane had something of a reputation for producing good football teams, and Jimmy looked forward to competing every Saturday, just like his heroes at Tottenham.

Until that period in his life he had been to schools with very little interest in football. Some schools didn't have an organised team, and those that did were managed by teachers with very little experience in the game. Now, at Smithwood Lane, Jimmy would have an opportunity to play the game properly, on proper pitches with proper referees and linesmen. It would be just like the real thing. No cobbled back streets for pitches, no break in play for tea and no more scuffed school trousers.

It wasn't long before he made his mark in schoolboy football. Team manager Mr Bateman, a man Greaves rates as having the best knowledge of football any schoolmaster could have, spotted the talent in his young pupil and played him up front for the first eleven. The young Jimmy had caught the eye with his pace and ability to dribble the ball around a mass of defenders before coolly putting it in the back of the net. Even at that age he was showing the promise that would soon attract scouts from London's big clubs. Jimmy made an impressive contribution in his first season, weighing in with a huge haul of goals as Smithwood Lane won the local schools league, but missed out on the cup double after losing in the final. Jimmy's efforts were rewarded with the captaincy the following year.

Sadly, his footballing education outpaced the academic side of things, with Jimmy preferring to dedicate his time to football rather than homework. It was an understandable decision to make. The prospects for boys growing up in the Dagenham area were very limited, and those who did manage to get a good education invariably ended up working in the Ford car plant anyway, where production was expanding as more and more people began to earn the sort of money that allowed them to afford a car. For the local lads, a life in the Ford factory was considered in the same light as a lifetime in Wormwood Scrubs; the Cortinas being produced by Ford at the time became affectionately known as 'Dagenham Dustbins'.

While football wasn't very well paid at this time, a career as a professional, turning out every week for Spurs, West Ham or Arsenal in front of thousands of fans, was far more interesting than a nine-to-five job in a hot factory, welding together car parts. Football was the desirable career path, although at this stage Jimmy's plans were far more short-term; he was still five years away from having to find a job for himself. A far more pressing concern lay immediately ahead: he had reached the age where he would have to leave the comfort of Smithwood Lane and look for a secondary school. More worrying than leaving behind friends, settling into a new environment and meeting new people was the fact that the nearest school, Kingswood Secondary Modern, a few miles down the road from Dagenham in Hainault, considered rugby as one of its stronger sports.

It was a prospect that worried Jimmy. Would he have to play rugby instead of football? How would he become a professional footballer if he had to play a sport he hated, rather than the game he loved? Jimmy wasn't going to take any chances. As he sat in the exam room before the start of his eleven-plus test, he knew what he had to do. He was going to deliberately fail the exam. In his own mind he knew he probably wouldn't have passed the test even if he had tried his hardest, but it was a risk he wasn't prepared to take. He flunked the test.

Despite this academic failure his family were determined that he still attend Kingswood, and the following autumn James Greaves enrolled as a new student. On his first day there he had a pleasant surprise. Fortunately, Kingswood's attitude to sport wasn't as strict as he had at first feared, and the school's love of rugby merely meant that Jimmy was allowed to shine when football came around. In what was a disappointing side (Kingswood didn't win a game in three seasons), Jimmy excelled, attracting attention from the local district side, Dagenham Schools. It was an opportunity that excited him and allowed him to team up with talented young players from the same area such as Terry Venables, Mike Harrison of Chelsea and John Smith, later of Spurs.

As the Kingswood side prepared for their fourth season together hopes, understandably, weren't high. Walking down one of the school's corridors at the start of a new term, Jimmy overheard a discussion about football among some of the teachers. The group was chatting about the forthcoming school league, each expressing his opinion on who would win it. Unsurprisingly, Kingswood wasn't even mentioned, which probably didn't surprise Jimmy, but disappointed him nevertheless. Maybe his schoolmasters should have shown more faith, for in their fourth season together Kingswood won the league without changing a player.

While Jimmy was beginning to enjoy a taste of success with Kingswood, the Dagenham Schools team gave him the opportunity to play with and compete against footballers of similar ability, and the youngster began to make a name for himself within the local football community. Terry Venables, a team-mate who had already played against Jimmy while playing for Dagenham Boys, was relishing the opportunity to play in the same side. Jimmy was turning out for his local U15 team at the time and had impressed Venables to such an extent that he began to hero-worship him. 'I was so impressed that I actually followed him home on the bus one day, without talking to him, just staring at him, in the hope of getting some clues about how to become that good. I did not get any answers and had a long walk home, after travelling miles past my stop.'

And it wasn't just the local boys who had taken notice of Jimmy Greaves' awesome talent. Several professional clubs were following his progress with interest as his career began to move along at a rapid speed. In 1955, at the age of fifteen, Jimmy began to represent London and Essex Boys, a team made up of the region's most exciting talent whose fixtures were a regular date in the diary for the scouts dedicated to scouring the capital for promising young footballers. Jimmy was a regular in the side and was receiving a fair amount of praise, but the attention, at the time, was the last thing on his mind.

The trials for the England Schoolboys team were just around the corner. Jimmy was desperate to pull on the white shirt of England and represent his country, but, unfortunately for him, the England selection process was still steeped in tradition and rules. According to the organisers it wasn't fair for boys from the same team to represent their country in consecutive years. The previous season another boy called Eddie Speight had been called up for a trial, and as a consequence Jimmy's ability was to be overlooked in favour of someone from a different team. The rejection frustrated Jimmy, who couldn't understand the logic of ignoring the best talent in the country in order to please every regional side. His disappointment was shortlived. After another impressive game from Jimmy for London Schools, his father was approached by a scout from Spurs who enquired as to whether Jimmy would be interested in a career playing professional football. Mr Greaves promptly told his son, who was delighted. Up until that point, a career as a professional footballer had just been a fantasy, a flight of fancy shared by every boy in his school. Now it was becoming a reality. A professional club had noticed his ability, and not just any old club, but Tottenham Hotspur, the team he'd supported as a boy! 'I'm not sure about this because it is hard to recall the exact date of a thought,' Greaves remembered later, 'but I believe that was the first time I reckoned I might earn my living at football. The idea tickled me pink. Until then I had merely thought in terms of playing football as many times a week as I could until I was too old to walk. Professional football, amateur football . . . the distinctions didn't mean anything.'

Bill Nicholson was also delighted. The former Spurs player, who had achieved so much under Arthur Rowe in the 'push and run' side, was now assisting his former manager with the coaching duties at White Hart Lane and was also impressed with the young Greaves' progress.

All the London clubs wanted him because he was a prolific scorer at junior level. I remember watching him play for London Schools at White Hart Lane. He had the natural instinct of the born goalscorer, which cannot be coached. Playing in the same side was another youngster of enormous promise, David Cliss. Cliss had more skill than Greaves, but he didn't make the grade. This happens often with schoolboys. A few go on and become good players, but so many fail. Everyone knew Greaves would succeed, however, because he had penetration. Arthur Rowe . . . anticipated that Greaves would sign as one of his apprentices.

Jimmy was hugely excited. He would soon be of an age when he'd have to start thinking about what to do when he left school. Unlike his friends, however, now he didn't have to dread the nine-to-five drudgery of work in a Dagenham Ford plant or worry about unemployment. Jimmy Greaves was going to sign for Spurs as an apprentice and make a name – and a fortune – for himself in the process. It was a dream come true.

Mr Greaves was invited to the club to meet Arthur Rowe. A meeting promptly took place during which Rowe explained the duties and responsibilities expected of a footballer, while discussing the wonderful opportunities for a talented youngster like Jimmy. Greaves senior was impressed. The wages were modest for an apprentice, but once he had become a fully fledged first-team player, his son could expect to play for a tidy sum. What's more, Tottenham struck him as an honest club with a genuine interest in the welfare of their young players. There had been no mention of backhanders or incentives for the family to entice Jimmy to the club. Spurs had played the whole thing straight, and the Greaves family were pleased by this and excited at the prospect of having a professional footballer in the household. More importantly for Mr Greaves, Spurs were an exciting side who played entertaining football, the sort of club at which his Jimmy could really make a name for himself.

So everything was set. Jimmy was to join Spurs as an apprentice after he'd finished his education. It promised to be the start of a glittering career as a professional footballer at White Hart Lane.

Or so everyone thought. Events were about to take a dramatic turn.

2 A Change of Heart

The world's greatest club and the world's greatest player just had to get together!

MR POPE, A.K.A. JIMMY THOMPSON, 1955

On a warm April afternoon in 1955 Jimmy Greaves sat in his front room considering the future. A few months before, everything had seemed so simple. He had been all set to leave school and turn up at White Hart Lane at the start of pre-season training to begin his apprenticeship. Both manager Arthur Rowe and his assistant Bill Nicholson had seen him play and had liked what they'd seen, and after a few meetings with the club Jimmy and his dad were happy that he should start a professional career with Tottenham. It had all seemed so uncomplicated. But now, with only a few more months at school remaining, things had taken a drastic twist, and Jimmy's position at White Hart Lane seemed a little precarious.

Arthur Rowe had fallen ill with the pressure of keeping Spurs out of the relegation zone and had been advised by doctors to stay clear of work for a few years until he had recovered. The rumour was that he might retire from the game completely. A new man, Jimmy Anderson, had been appointed because of his experience as a manager who was good with the more office-related side of running a big football club, while Bill Nicholson was appointed to take over the team's coaching duties. Because of his lack of experience, Anderson was concerned that caring for all the young apprentices taken on by his predecessor would prove too difficult. Looking after the first team was a full-time job in itself, without having to worry about a bunch of young hopefuls at the same time. Spurs still wanted Greaves, but Jimmy wasn't sure if he wanted to be at a club that couldn't promise him full-time attention.

He slumped back in his chair, still considering his future, when there was a loud knock at the front door. Scrambling out of his chair, Jimmy ran out of the lounge to answer it. Turning the handle, he pulled the door ajar to be greeted by a smiling man in a smart suit and bowler hat. Taking the hat off his head and forcing it into Jimmy's arms, the stranger strode through the door, past the youngster and through the house until he found the kitchen. Jimmy was shocked. Who was this character? If he was a salesman, he was certainly pushy. Recovering his composure, he chased after him, fearing the worst and remembering his mum was in the kitchen. But it was too late. His bemused mother had already been accosted.

'Put the kettle on, ma, and we'll have a cup of tea,' said the man in a chirpy cockney accent. He seemed too inoffensive to be a threat, so a still confused Mrs Greaves reached for the kettle. 'I want to talk about your Jim over a cuppa,' he continued by way of an explanation.

By this point Jimmy was interested. He was even more interested when the mysterious character revealed he was a football scout who had been watching the young Greaves for some time. He introduced himself as Mr Pope, but that wasn't his real name, he explained. It was merely a pseudonym to deceive several London clubs who had been tailing boys in the Dagenham area, only for 'Mr Pope' to steal them from under their noses for another club. That club was Chelsea, and they were, Mr Pope said, very interested in one Jimmy Greaves, who had certainly turned a few heads with his performances for London Schools.

Jimmy and his mother sat down as Mr Pope began to wax lyrical about Chelsea's potential, the standard of football at the club and the wonderful things that

Jimmy could achieve there. Chelsea were made to sound remarkably better than the average First Division outfit they had been recently (although at that time they were in a good position to take the title), and Spurs were described as if they were nothing more than a ramshackle non-League club. Jimmy was impressed, but he certainly wasn't going to make a decision without consulting his father. Would Mr Pope mind waiting?

'Of course not,' he replied. 'We can talk more about your future at a certain south-west London club!'

They waited while Mr Pope chattered constantly. He certainly had charm, and Jimmy was much taken by him, but he knew his father would be a very different story. Greaves senior was very keen on Spurs and, as an honourable man, wanted to fulfil their promise to the club. Persuading his father to change his mind would be a difficult job. Even for Mr Pope.

His father soon arrived home from work and was introduced to the stranger. Mr Pope repeated his impressive spiel, waving his hands about theatrically to indicate the size and ambition of Chelsea, but Greaves senior wasn't as easily moved as his wide-eyed son.

'I'll think it over,' he said. 'Come back next week.'

Greaves' father was concerned. Who was this Mr Pope? What could Chelsea offer that a club of Spurs' size couldn't? And why all the mystery and intrigue? Quickly, he decided to investigate Mr Pope himself. His son seemed keen on the idea of moving to Chelsea – probably because they were about to become First Division champions – but he didn't want anyone to let Jimmy down. Spurs had been honest with him, and he wanted to be honest with them, but if Chelsea were going to make his son happy, then maybe they were worth considering.

He left the house and went round to see Les Allen's father, who lived a few roads away. Les had already signed for Chelsea and was doing well as an apprentice; would he happen to know anything about this mysterious scout masquerading as a Mr Pope? Both Les and his father were unaware of a Mr Pope, but could testify to the quality of Chelsea Football Club. That was it as far as Greaves senior was concerned. He knew his son had been taken in by this mysterious charmer and could feel his enthusiasm for Tottenham waning. It annoyed him, but he knew Jimmy was only young and it was natural enough for him to be fickle. If Chelsea were a good club and Jimmy was keen on going there, then that was enough for him. More importantly, he didn't want his son to become the subject of a bidding war. He was aware of how some football clubs operated and didn't like the underhand methods they used to convince young players to join their squads. Sure, a cash incentive might seem a nice idea to the parents of some footballers, but it just felt wrong to the Greaves family.

Jimmy was convinced Stamford Bridge was the place for him. But if he was sure after his initial meeting with Mr Pope, his decision was positively cemented the following week. Mr Pope – who eventually introduced himself as Jimmy Thompson after a succession of meetings – had been round to the Greaves household on several occasions, much to the amusement of the family. It was only spring after all. If Pope – or Thompson – was keen on him now, what would he be like when summer arrived and Jimmy was able to leave school and sign forms with a professional club?

And West Ham had also begun to take an interest in Jimmy Greaves; manager Ted Fenton had also put in a personal appearance at the Greaves home. But although they were the local side and had one or two handy players, Jimmy had never been taken by the Hammers and remained unimpressed by their attempts to sign him. His father was also reluctant to sign anything with the club. They were a Second Division side after all, and Jimmy had attracted interest from far bigger fish.

After several weeks of deliberation, discussion and almost daily visits from Thompson, Greaves' father allowed his son to make his own decision and inform 'Mr Pope'. Jimmy was delighted. Although he could sense his dad's disappointment, he was convinced his future lay at Stamford Bridge. They were now the champions, and a number of his friends and other players he knew were already there or in the process of signing for the club. The following evening, when Thompson arrived on their doorstep yet again, Jimmy greeted him with the good news.

'I want to sign for Chelsea,' he said.

Thompson smiled broadly. 'You'll never regret this, my boy,' he beamed. 'You have my word on that. The world's greatest club and the world's greatest player just had to get together. I should like to take you to the ground personally on Monday morning to meet Mr Drake. See you at Liverpool Street station. I'll meet you under the clock.'

Jimmy was taken aback. Ted Drake was one of the most respected managers in English football at the time, and he was going to see him on Monday. For the next couple of nights he fantasised about his meeting with one of British football's most famous faces, how he was going to be told he was a great young talent and how much Drake wanted Jimmy Greaves to sign for Chelsea. Monday was going to be a wonderful day, and Jimmy couldn't wait, although he was a little apprehensive. It was all happening so quickly.

Despite his nerves, Jimmy was at Liverpool Street with plenty of time to spare that Monday. Wandering around the station looking out for Jimmy Thompson, he began to recognise a few familiar faces milling around the shops. They weren't people he knew from school or home, but young boys, all around his age, who had either played with or against London Schools or one of his Sunday sides. It seemed a little strange, but they were probably meeting for a game or a trial or a friendly match somewhere, so he didn't give it a second thought. Then he saw Jimmy Thompson pushing his way through the crowds of commuters, stopping every so often to talk to someone, the familiar bowler hat bobbing up and down above the heads of other passengers walking along the concourse.

The truth suddenly hit Jimmy. The boys he had seen at the station weren't meeting up for a game, they were all meeting the same man: 'Mr Pope'. Thompson had convinced all of them to sign for Chelsea and was rounding them up at Liverpool Street station!

'Ah, there you are!' shouted Thompson as he got round to Jimmy, delighted at being reunited with his 'star' player. 'There you go,' he said, forcing a mint and a ticket to Fulham Broadway station into Jimmy's hand before leading all the boys off in a procession to Chelsea Football Club. It wouldn't be quite the exclusive introduction to Ted Drake that Jimmy had expected, but it was still an adventure of sorts.

The group was led from central London right up to the corridor outside Ted Drake's office. The boys sat patiently, each waiting for the door to creak open and a voice to summon them individually inside. Strangely, the boys would leave via another door which led to a billiards room, so nobody could tell whether the meeting was going to be a pleasant or a nerve-racking experience.

Jimmy sat nervously. This was his big moment. He watched the door as the handle turned again and Jimmy Thompson popped his head outside, beckoning him in typically dramatic fashion. Jimmy looked around before making his way sheepishly into the office. Ted Drake sat there, Thompson standing to one side, beaming broadly. Jimmy was introduced, informed of his duties as a groundstaff boy and ushered upstairs to the billiards room to meet Dickie Foss, Chelsea's junior team manager.

Foss was a good coach and had built up something of a reputation as a hard manager, but the truth was a little different. Jimmy was impressed by his approach. Rather than the stern taskmaster of legend, Foss was a fair man with the ability to encourage and praise his players, while at the same time keeping their feet firmly on the floor. Jimmy soon signed the schoolboy forms that would see him earning the modest sum of £5 per week as a groundstaff boy. And while the sum may have been a small one compared to the lucrative contracts signed today by youth players in the Premiership, a fiver was a huge amount to a fifteen-year-old in the mid-1950s. Jimmy was delighted.

What's more, his father was also happy. His gravest concerns – that his son would be the focus of a bidding war between big London clubs, that his family would be assailed by less than scrupulous offerings (under-the-table deals were common when trying to attract the best young talent, and clubs would often encourage families to sign their sons away with cash or 'presents' such as furniture or TV sets; indeed, some families literally auctioned off their talented offspring) – had proved groundless. Chelsea and Mr Pope had played everything above board.

It came as something of a surprise, then, when another mysterious character turned up on the Greaves doorstep with a brown envelope, shortly after Jimmy had signed for Chelsea. In it was a wad of money. Jimmy's father was taken aback. No one had even so much as tried to bribe him before his son had signed for Chelsea, so he felt the cash must be something more in the line of a present rather than a 'bung'. He counted the money in the envelope: £50, all of it in Irish £5 notes. It wasn't the hugest amount of money and was nothing compared to the cash thrown at some players' families, but, satisfied that the money was not being used to sway a decision in any way because his son had already signed for a club, it was a gift that was warmly accepted by Greaves Senior, with a clear conscience.

Everyone seemed pleased with the deal, and by the end of May 1955, with the papers signed and sealed, Jimmy Greaves was about to take his first few steps into the glamorous world of professional football. He was also on the threshold of learning a few harsh lessons about life outside the school gates.

3 The Stamford Bridge Nightmare

I suddenly decided that professional football was not for me. I was bored stiff.

JIMMY GREAVES, 1972

Jimmy Greaves' formative years at Stamford Bridge were not the most comfortable. In fact, they were positively miserable. An apprenticeship was not the glamorous experience Greaves and his school friends had perceived it to be and he became disillusioned after only one month at the club. During the summer the apprentices had found themselves painting the ground, but in the autumn the training started and the real work could begin at last. After a morning of working around the ground, carrying out repairs and reseeding the pitch, the youth team would be taken away for training in the afternoon, and it was here that Greaves could really express himself.

The striker quickly formed a rapport with youth team coach Dickie 'Fossie' Foss. Foss was a classic man manager, a coach who would put his arm around a player who was feeling low and within minutes have him feeling like the best footballer in the world. He was also a realist who liked to keep his players' heads out of the clouds. If Chelsea won 5–0, Fossie would want to know why his side hadn't scored an extra five goals. It was important to him that his sides always strived to go one better, and any delusions of grandeur were quickly wiped out within five minutes of a debriefing in the dressing room following a victory.

Greaves respected Foss. Here was the first manager who had ever attempted to teach him and hone his skills. Before now, Greaves had always been self-taught, relying on information from schoolmasters who never really knew how best to nurture a player of his undoubted ability. But rather than remould Greaves' mode of play or alter his technique, Foss merely improved on what was already an effective style, sharpening the strengths that were there in abundance and ironing out the weaknesses. It was an educational process that encouraged Greaves.

The reasons for Greaves' unhappiness lay in the reality that, despite the fact he was constantly improving as a player under Foss's direction, he couldn't break into the youth team's starting eleven. It quickly became apparent that Chelsea had too many youngsters, no doubt due to the strenuous efforts of Jimmy Thompson the previous season. In fact, so great were the numbers that it was impossible to train all the boys together; sessions would be split between the mornings and afternoons, with Greaves involved in the afternoon shift. And among the crowds Chelsea had a number of impressive youngsters on their books, all of them vying for a place in the youth team. Greaves soon found himself sitting out the action on Saturday afternoons.

The main obstacle for Greaves was a player called Peter Brabrook. Brabrook was a much respected player at the club and had impressed Foss with his ability in front of goal. Despite the fact that he was a regular in Chelsea's first and reserve teams, Brabrook was still eligible to play for the youth side, and Greaves found himself sitting on the bench for the entire 1955/56 Youth Cup campaign. Whenever Brabrook was available for selection, Greaves was omitted. It was a rejection the fifteen-year-old found difficult to cope with, and rather than attempt to oust his striking rival from his first-team spot, he simply resigned himself to the fact that Brabrook was a better player, that there was no way past him. Still, when Greaves played he would invariably impress, and the striker began his Chelsea career in typically dramatic fashion, scoring after only one minute on his debut against Watford's junior side in a 5–1 win.

But even when he was playing Greaves was unhappy, shocked by the levels of apathy at the club. Chelsea had won the First Division title the previous season and were reflecting on their glorified status as League champions. Rather than take steps to ensure the title was retained, Ted Drake and his team seemed content merely to bask in the limelight. The mood at the club was not dissimilar to that of a summer school; players came and went as they pleased. It was an attitude that worried Greaves. If Chelsea were champions, why did they seem so unconcerned about the possibility that they might lose the crown? Why was everyone so complacent? And why did the youth team seem to train harder than the first-team professionals?

From the moment he'd joined the club, Greaves had been immersed in the relaxed atmosphere at Stamford Bridge. On reporting for his first day's duties, he'd been handed two weeks' wages and told to take a fortnight off. The 1954/55 season had only recently finished and the club wasn't ready to take on a new batch of youngsters just yet, so Greaves was asked to return in two weeks' time when he would begin his duties in earnest. For a fortnight Greaves had hung around the local park with friends, kicking a ball around, waiting to start a new career, while his mates attempted to find work. Finally, the day had come. Strolling into the club, Greaves had been greeted by Foss, only to be told that he had to come back in two days' time because the club still wasn't ready to start preparations for the next season. Life at Chelsea from the start seemed to be the life of Riley.

But even at the age of fifteen, the lethargy around him frustrated Greaves. What's more, he was soon learning the harsh realities of life as an apprentice. Jimmy Thompson hadn't told him the days at Stamford Bridge would involve hours of back-breaking work before the luxurious afternoons out on the training

ground could begin. As far as Thompson was concerned, life as a junior player at Chelsea Football Club
was one long holiday, a life of leisure. Sure, you might
have to paint the odd pillar here or sweep a terrace
there, but really, life as a youngster was one long picnic
– a few years of developing a football talent before
being thrust into the limelight as a first-team player.
Sadly for Greaves and his family, Thompson had
neglected to mention that life as an apprentice would
also involve a lot of hard manual work for little thanks.

Greaves felt cheated. A few months back, according
to Thompson he was a star in the making, but the only
starring role Greaves had at Stamford Bridge was in his
official capacity as the club's drinks-maker. He was
cooped up in a stuffy office all day, running errands
and doing chores for the staff at the club. The reality
was that he was being used as a gofer rather than 'the
greatest player in the world' at 'the greatest club in the
world', as Thompson had so colourfully described his
signing-on at Chelsea. His lowest ebb came when he
was asked to help put up a new set of floodlights with
some of his team-mates. It was a task he later described
as 'cheap labour', and gradually it forced him into
making a decision about his future. Just one year on
from signing his forms as an apprentice, at the end of
the 1955/56 season, Jimmy Greaves decided he wanted
to give up the dream of being a professional footballer
and asked Foss for his cards.

I still wanted to play as much as ever, but some of
the brightness had gone off the glamour. Bluntly, I
was browned off. Being an office boy didn't help.
After making your thousandth cup of tea you begin
to wonder where you are going. Jimmy Thompson
had forgotten to mention that I would spend more
time boosting the tea company's profits than I would
playing football.

That was when I decided I would play as an
amateur. I went and saw Dickie Foss and told him I

wanted my cards. I told him I was going to get a job outside football and play as an amateur. Fossy tried to talk me out of it. He was one of the few people in those days who thought I had a future in the game. He didn't succeed, and I collected my cards and went.

Greaves had made up his mind, despite protestations from the club. He wanted to go somewhere where he would be wanted. He was tired of being treated like a lackey. If football wasn't the way to fame and fortune, then he would find another career that could take him to the riches he felt he deserved.

After flicking through situations vacant in the local paper, he quickly found a job that would suit him. A local publishing company was looking for a messenger boy with exactly the credentials and level of experience Greaves had at the time. Sure, it was a similar job to the one at Chelsea, but at least he had a clear opportunity to progress and improve himself. And he was determined he wouldn't be treated badly or overlooked like he had been at Chelsea. He would be a successful businessman in no time.

He promptly applied for the job and received a response within days. His application had impressed and his new employers wanted him to start immediately. Greaves was delighted. He hadn't realised a fresh start would be so easy to make, and he accepted the company's offer. The salary was a modest one, but in a matter of years he would probably have his own office and would be making more money than any professional footballer could ever dream of.

Like his initial dreams as an apprentice at Chelsea, his image of life in the City proved to be a false one. There were no quick bucks to be made, there were no shortcuts to unimaginable wealth. And what's more, Greaves did indeed find himself carrying out the same demeaning tasks he'd been asked to perform at Stamford Bridge. One week later he was back in Dickie

Foss's office, pleading for another chance to work at Chelsea.

Greaves, understandably, was unsure of what Foss's reaction might be. Would he be pleased to see him, or would he tell him his chance had gone, that he would have to find another club or, worse still, another career? Remarkably, Foss was very calm. Rather than lecture his errant player on the error of his ways while informing him of the countless boys who would kill for the opportunity to be in Greaves' shoes, Foss simply nodded and accepted him back into the fold. He was well aware that any criticism or mockery could easily bruise Greaves' confidence at a time when he was wondering whether football was the profession for him. To reprimand him now could cause irreparable damage. As far as Foss knew, Ted Drake wasn't even aware that Greaves had left, so there was no need to rock the boat. And besides, he was pleased Greaves had returned.

Immediate success followed his return. His brief period of absence from football had given the sixteen-year-old what can only be described as a kick up the backside. Greaves' form improved dramatically: he scored 114 goals for the Youth side during the 1956/57 season, including seven in one match and eight goals in another. The main reason for this success was that he'd finally been given a chance to play regularly in the youth team. Peter Brabrook, who had long commanded the coveted striker's spot in the Chelsea youth side, was now too old to play for them and was making regular appearances in the first team. Greaves had been given an extended run in the starting line-up as a result and was beginning to show the form that had impressed many who watched him as a schoolboy.

This phenomenal strike rate didn't go unnoticed, and the first-team manager began to watch Greaves with interest. Here was a player who could evidently walk around defences with ease, and he was only sixteen! What would he be like with some first-team experience under his belt? Before the season was over, Drake made the decision that Greaves was good enough to sign full professional terms with the club.

In February 1957, under the instructions of Drake, Jimmy Thompson made a return visit to the Greaves household – this time with a different agenda. The young Greaves had just turned seventeen, making him eligible to sign for whoever he wanted. Chelsea had lost talented youngsters before to rival clubs and didn't want to make the same mistake with Greaves. Thompson was typically enthusiastic. Once again, Chelsea were described as the greatest club in the world, despite languishing in the middle of the table ever since being crowned as champions. The opportunities for a youth player were fantastic, Thompson went on, but the opportunities for a full professional footballer at Stamford Bridge were out of this world.

Greaves stalled. The one thing he wanted more than anything else at that time was an England Youth cap. To be eligible for a call-up a player had to be an amateur, and by signing professional forms with Chelsea there and then, any chance of representing his country at this level would disappear for ever. Thompson understood. After all, it wasn't as if the boy was holding out for more money or waiting for another club. Still, the longer Greaves mused over his dilemma, the more desperate the club became. Thompson was soon making regular visits to the Greaves doorstep.

What amused Greaves more than Thompson's eagerness was the change in the people he worked with at the club. Office workers and coaching staff who had previously looked down their noses at him and ordered him to make tea or fetch cigarettes and newspapers were now going out of their way to make sure he was comfortable at work. Realising his age and standing as a promising young player placed him in a powerful position, and this was as much a reason as any for Greaves' delaying tactics. He'd known virtually from the outset that he wanted to sign full terms, but what harm could come of milking the situation a little bit? It was only a little bit of fun. But by May, Ted Drake was at his wits' end. Greaves had to sign for Chelsea, and Thompson was sent once again to bring back his signature.

At the time of Thompson's dispatch, Greaves was walking down the Fulham Road with his then girlfriend (and later wife) Irene. In the distance, bobbing and weaving his way past assorted walkers and shoppers with great urgency, Greaves spotted Thompson, the familiar bowler hat propped up on his head. Greaves knew that something was wrong immediately and braced himself for a dramatic outburst. Thompson stopped abruptly in front of him and grabbed his arm.

'Jimmy,' he said sternly. 'Mr Drake wants to see you in his office. Now.'

Greaves looked at Irene, then back at Thompson. It was unlikely the scout had even seen her. Greaves was annoyed. While Thompson was a likeable individual, his abruptness and short-sightedness were at times very irritating.

'I've got my girlfriend here,' he replied. 'I can't come now.'

Thompson looked Irene up and down, acknowledging her for the first time. 'I'll look after her,' he said to Jimmy, before turning to Irene and pointing to a café down the road. 'You go and wait in there. He'll only be ten minutes.'

Greaves was infuriated. Barging into his house and demanding tea was bad enough. The endless house calls to ensure he hadn't signed for another club were a constant nuisance. But now Thompson was insulting his girlfriend. Greaves decided to put his foot down.

'No. I'm not coming.'

Thompson flashed him a look of disbelief, followed by a hard, dramatic glare. His tone of voice was slow and stern. Greaves knew he was serious.

'Jimmy,' he said, slowly emphasising each word, 'this is your future.'

Greaves nodded. He knew he had played the club for time and that enough was enough, but he still had one more trick up his sleeve. If Chelsea wanted him that badly, surely they could push a little bit of extra cash his way? He knew of players receiving under-the-counter cash when they signed professional forms with a club, so why shouldn't he make a little bit of money out of his signature?

'It was when it dawned on me how much Chelsea wanted me to turn professional that I began to think about stinging them for some cash,' Greaves recalled. 'I had heard about how players at other clubs had got away with illegal payments and had made up my mind to put some pressure on Chelsea. I went into Ted Drake's office feeling a little like a hold-up man. All that was missing was a mask and a gun!'

So Greaves went with Thompson, determined to try his luck yet again. Approaching the manager's office, he was nervous. He wasn't sure how he should point out the fact that he needed more money. Would it be better to be subtle, or should he just come straight out with his demands? Greaves decided to play it by ear, with the intention of applying some pressure if necessary. Drake greeted Greaves politely as he walked into the office, before outlining the fact that Greaves had impressed many people at the club and he wanted him to sign for the club as a professional footballer. Greaves knew it was only small talk, but listened intently. Drake pointed out he would be earning £17 a week as a professional, with a £2 win bonus. Even in those days, £17 was not a vast amount of money. Unlike the modern athlete, footballers by trade weren't the most highly paid people in the world. Greaves knew the time had come to apply the pressure.

'I don't actually earn a lot of money at the moment,' stuttered Greaves. 'I'm a little short of cash.'

It was very far from the ruthless ultimatum he had envisaged delivering. He knew he had to be subtle, but his hint fell on deaf ears. Drake scratched his head and slumped back in his chair. It was a complaint he had heard countless times before, but a young footballer could never expect to make hundreds of pounds overnight. He seemed unaware that Greaves was angling for a cash extra there and then.

'We all have to start at the bottom of the ladder,' he began, frowning.

Greaves knew the manager had misunderstood his intentions. He was also irritated by this bottom-of-the-ladder spiel, which he'd heard on countless occasions. If Chelsea wanted him that badly they would have to show it. A weekly wage of £17 was a nice amount for a boy of his age (he was only on £7 at the time), but he would have to be blunt if he wanted to see the cash he felt he deserved.

'I've been thinking of joining another club,' he blurted out.

There was an awkward silence. Drake had been facing away from Greaves in a swivel chair, looking out of his office as he delivered his humbling speech. Now he spun the chair around and was staring directly at his youth player.

'Jimmy!' he shouted, throwing a pencil on to the table in front of him. 'If you don't sign for Chelsea I shall resign as manager right now!'

Drake's reaction shocked Greaves. In his mind he had expected him to nod and give him a wink before sliding a brown envelope stuffed full of notes towards him. He hadn't pictured an outburst like this.

Before the echo of the words had died away I had reached a shaking hand across the desk, grabbed the pen and form and written my name faster than it has ever been written before. It looked as if it had been written by a man of 95 in the middle of doing the twist. In one split second I visualised Chelsea without a manager, perhaps the club finished and the ground turned over to allotments – and all because I had asked for a bit on the side!

I couldn't get out of the office fast enough. But before I did get away, Ted Drake said: 'Jimmy, don't ever take illegal money in this game. You're stuck with it for the rest of your life. It can follow you around and ruin you years afterwards.' He was very decent about my attempt to hold him up, and the advice was good. I must have given a bit of a joke performance, really.

Despite failing to strongarm Drake, Greaves had gone from being a downbeat apprentice on £5 a week, picking up an extra £2 per week on turning sixteen, to a young man in the position of being able to claim the princely sum of £17 for the luxury of playing football every Saturday afternoon. It was like a dream come true. But more importantly for Greaves and for Chelsea, the seventeen-year-old was about to become an overnight sensation.

4 The Teenager's Fan Club

*The boy is a natural. He is the greatest youngster I have
ever played against.*

DANNY BLANCHFLOWER, 1957

A few months after signing pro forms at Stamford Bridge,
a seventeen-year-old Jimmy Greaves was thrown in at
the deep end. At 2.50 p.m. on 23 August, the day of the
opening fixtures of the 1957/58 season, he sat in the
Chelsea dressing room at White Hart Lane, having been
drafted into the first team. Only ten minutes to kick-off,
he thought. Better start preparing myself. Through the
walls of the changing room he could hear the buzz of the
crowd outside. Spurs v. Chelsea was always a big game.
The fans loved a London derby, especially Spurs and
Chelsea, and especially on the first day of the season.
And today the crowd were in for a bit of extra excitement.
Jimmy Greaves was to make his Chelsea debut.

Even he was shocked that he'd been selected to play
in the opening game of Chelsea's League campaign. It
only seemed like yesterday that he'd signed the contract in Ted Drake's office after cheekily asking for a
cash bonus before he'd even kicked a ball in professional football. Now he was about to make his debut
against one of the biggest clubs in the country, and a
club he'd nearly joined as well. Spurs already had stars
on their books and were sure to have a good season, but
how would Greaves get on, especially when he knew
that the immaculate Spurs skipper Danny Blanchflower
would be man-marking him?

To be fair, Greaves had been steeled for this moment
during the summer break. As soon as he'd become a

professional at Chelsea, the team had been whisked away to Holland for a summer tournament. He'd been shocked to be included at such an early stage, but it was an enjoyable experience. He'd been to Holland a few times to play football, but this time was different. This time he was with the Chelsea first team. He felt important. More impressively, he'd jumped straight into the first team without making a single reserve appearance, so he was sure the club and Ted Drake had faith in him. But could he repay that faith?

It had all happened so fast. One minute he was making tea for the directors at the club, the next he was representing their team abroad. He knew he'd played well and deserved a place, but nonetheless felt like something of an outsider trying to break in. The players in the squad were all experienced pros, except for Michael Harrison, who had played once for the first team and was a regular in the reserves. But even reserve games amounted to experience in abundance compared to what Greaves had under his belt. He got a game or two while overseas and felt he hadn't done himself any harm, but he certainly wasn't expecting such a positive move from the manager.

Ted Drake had taken his new signing to one side following the Holland tour and told him his plans. The manager intended to start Greaves in the first game of the season if everything went according to plan during the club's second trip to Holland the following month. Of course, everything did, and Greaves, who was still only seventeen, was considered experienced enough to make the starting line-up for the game against Spurs.

Fortunately he didn't suffer from nerves. Big games and crowds had never bothered him. Some players he knew would spend days fretting before the most minor of games, let alone a League debut in front of 50,000 fans, but for Greaves it was another match against another team. Working yourself up into a state never does you any good, thought Greaves, and he wasn't going to start worrying now. In fact, the only person who became nervous whenever he played was his girlfriend Irene, whom he soon planned to marry. But she was more concerned about the possibility of his picking up a nasty injury rather than putting in a bad performance.

Greaves looked at the clock on the wall. Only a few minutes to go. He adjusted his shorts, a pair of long, baggy ones he always insisted on wearing whenever he played. They were unusual for the time because the fashion was to wear tight shorts, and he received a fair bit of stick from his team-mates about them. It didn't bother him. There were no superstitious reasons for wearing them, he just liked the feel of them. Some people thought he was wearing them as a gimmick, but the truth was that on his first day at Chelsea he was kitted out with a pair that were too big for him. Although they were too large, they were so comfortable that he decided to carry on wearing them, despite the mickey-taking.

The other players got out of their seats. As he prepared to leave the dressing room with the others, someone patted him on the back. 'All the best,' the voice said as they walked through the tunnel. It was the nearest thing to advice Greaves had heard all day. At junior level they had received tactical briefings from Fossie and information on how to play against a particular team before every match. In the first team there was no such procedure. In fact, everything was so much more relaxed. There'd been no team meeting, no game plan. Nothing. Greaves was surprised. Were they just expected to go out there and play? It was to be the moment of reckoning.

Ninety minutes later, Greaves' concerns were a distant memory. Chelsea had drawn a game they'd always looked likely to lose. Spurs had dominated for the majority of the match, playing a young Chelsea team off the park. But more importantly than picking up a vital point, Greaves had scored the equaliser. He was delighted, but knew it was important to keep his feet on the ground and not sound too big-headed. He'd dribbled the ball past three players before passing the ball to the side of the keeper and into the back of the net, but he wasn't going to make too much of it. Nonetheless, he'd scored what was later to become regarded as a typical Greaves goal.

The Spurs manager, Bill Nicholson, was very impressed by Greaves' performance and described the seventeen-year-old's goal as 'unforgettable'. Skipper Danny Blanchflower was also taken by the teenager, having struggled to keep tabs on him throughout the match. Blanchflower was rarely found wanting against strikers, preferring to out-think rather than out-muscle them, but even he'd found Greaves' quick running and incisive movement a handful. Greaves was relieved he'd been marked by Blanchflower rather than a more physical defender. The Irishman was renowned for his grace and skill rather than the ability to kick opponents into the stands, and Greaves came away from his debut unscathed. He knew that in the coming months other defenders would not be so gracious towards him, especially if he performed like that every week.

If Greaves had been relatively pleased with his performance, the national press were positively enthusiastic. They had found a new star to rank alongside some of the greatest strikers in English football. 'Jimmy Greaves gave the greatest show I have ever seen from a young player in his League debut,' gushed Desmond Hackett of the *Daily Express* the following day. 'And I have seen the juvenile performances of soccer starlets Johnny Haynes and Duncan Edwards.' Things had got off to a fairytale start and the press were determined to hang on to his coat tails, making sure they followed every dramatic twist of his life in professional football.

They didn't have to wait long to write the next headline. Greaves scored six times in the first eight matches, waltzing around defenders and displaying a predatory instinct that had fans and sport editors drooling. After only a handful of games in a Chelsea shirt, in September Greaves was picked to represent the England U23 side for two games against Bulgaria and Romania. It was here that Greaves was to play alongside Fulham's Johnny Haynes for the first time in a partnership that was to prove fruitful at full international level. Greaves' best performance came against the Bulgarians: he scored twice and missed a penalty for his hat-trick as England crushed them 6–2 at Stamford Bridge.

All the while his game improved dramatically, and soon the press were clamouring for his selection in the full England squad for the 1958 World Cup in Sweden. But despite his confidence in front of goal, Greaves knew his first full international tournament was still a few years off, although the praise being heaped upon him was welcome. And as if to prove the point of the reticent England selectors, and dismaying headline writers everywhere, Greaves' goals suddenly dried up.

At that point, things began going wrong. My form started to slip away from me, the goals weren't coming. There was no deep secret about it. I was simply too young to keep it up the way I had been going.

So Drake called me in and told me he was resting me for ten days. I was being dropped, but so gently that it wouldn't have cracked an eggshell. As it was, ten days got stretched from mid-October to Christmas, but that was reasonable enough – Les Stubbs was playing well in my place, and it took me longer to shake off my tiredness than expected . . . That was the only time I was dropped by Chelsea. Needless to say, that break was enough to finish off my prospects of playing in the World Cup, not that I was ready for it in any case. Instead, I watched the matches on television.

Despite the disappointment of his enforced absence from the Chelsea line-up, Greaves' return to the first team was as dramatic as his debut. Two months away from competitive football had had a positive effect on the striker, who came out for his return game against Portsmouth on Boxing Day like a greyhound out of the traps, scoring four goals in front of an ecstatic Stamford Bridge crowd as Chelsea swept aside the visitors with a 7–4 thrashing. 'The phenomenal Jimmy Greaves gave Portsmouth a Christmas socking with four of Chelsea's seven goals at Stamford Bridge,' wrote Peter Lorenzo of the *Daily Herald* the following morning. 'It was a case of many happy returns for Greaves, who had been rested by manager Ted Drake because "he's too good to hurry".'

Those who felt Greaves' early streak was a flash in the pan were to be disappointed. The young striker scored 22 goals in this first season with the Chelsea first team. Ted Drake realised he had a very talented prospect on his hands, despite the club's disappointing eleventh place in the First Division. It was the beginning of a fruitful four-year relationship with the Stamford Bridge club.

During his second year in the first team, Greaves became the League's top scorer, notching up 32 goals, but it was a traumatic time for the eighteen-year-old. He had just married his childhood sweetheart, Irene, and was receiving a fair amount of patronising lectures from the club about it. Rather than encouraging Greaves to settle down into a relaxed family life instead of spending his time in clubs and dance halls, Chelsea saw Greaves' early marriage as a worrying sign. The club was concerned that the new way of life would take his mind off his performances on the football pitch, especially when things weren't going so well at home. It was a lot to take for someone so young, and Chelsea's attitude angered Greaves. Here he was, settling down into a sensible way of life, and the club was tutting and shaking heads behind his back. Surely it would be better for him as a footballer to be having a relaxed evening with his wife rather than spending most evenings out on the town with the other single lads in the team?

Once again, Greaves made up his mind on the issue. If the club felt his marriage to Irene was going to have a negative influence on his game, then he would do everything he could to prove them wrong. Finishing the 1958/59 season with 32 goals was a good retort, as was his regular appearance in the England U23 side. By the time Greaves had scored on his full England debut against Peru in May 1959, the Chelsea backroom staff were eating their words (despite the fact that England had been beaten 4–1). Come the 1959/60 season, Greaves was considered an established first-team regular and one of the most feared strikers in the League, but despite the fact he had risen to prominence so quickly and had built himself a fearsome reputation, he was not happy at Chelsea.

He enjoyed the style of football encouraged by Drake and had a great rapport with the coaching and playing staff, but he found himself becoming increasingly frustrated at the club's slack attitude to progress. If he had been concerned by Chelsea's apparent satisfaction with mid-table mediocrity as a youth player, he now found their backward attitude positively depressing. The general mood in the dressing room before the game was one of apathy, while positive vibes in terms of getting results were almost non-existent. Nobody expected to win a game, and if Chelsea did pick up two points, then it was little more than a nice way to spend the afternoon. Defeats were treated with a sense of humour, and the atmosphere in the Chelsea dressing room was often more light-hearted than in the winning team's.

In short, Chelsea had become something of a joke; as they moved feebly about the middle and bottom half of the table, they were frequently the target of fun for most of the club comedians across London. For the players, it was a nice, relaxed way to spend the week. The fans, however, were pulling their hair out in frustration, and Greaves had nothing but sympathy for them. In five years, Chelsea had gone from being League champions to a team that in attitude and outlook resembled nothing more than a pub side.

More worrying for Greaves was the fact that, even allowing for their mid-table qualities, the club was showing very little sign of progress. First Division football at the time was being increasingly dominated by Manchester United: the Old Trafford side had picked up the League championship in 1956 and 1957 and finished runners-up in 1959. Led by Matt Busby, it was the side that quickly became nicknamed the 'Busby Babes', featuring a blend of talent and youth most of which was tragically wiped out in the 1958 Munich air disaster, including such names as Duncan Edwards, Bill Whelan and Roger Byrne. A small nucleus for a future side had, however, survived the crash, Bobby Charlton, Ray Wood and Bill Foulkes among them.

Chelsea manager Ted Drake had become obsessed with the idea of putting together a young side in a similar vein to Matt Busby's successful team at Old Trafford. It was his dream to build a team that could go on and win trophies for years to come and bring the glory days back to Chelsea. However, Drake's plan had one flaw. Like so many media tags, the 'Busby Babes' nickname wasn't strictly true: United were actually fielding a team which carefully combined youth and experience, rather than a rag-tag mob of children barely out of school and still wet behind the ears. Drake, though, with hope in his heart, was sending out a team of boys with very little experience of playing at the top level. If a player caught his eye in the youth team he would be drafted into the first team without any introduction to reserve-team football. It was a little like sending lambs to the slaughter.

Chelsea did succeed in picking up a nickname – 'Drake's Ducklings' – but, unlike their rivals from Manchester, Drake's team carried on struggling to pick up results. The problem for the team wasn't necessarily the talent, which was there in abundance, but the experience. Older, more physical sides soon realised that the way to beat Chelsea was to out-muscle them on the park, and the inexperienced Stamford Bridge side would often find themselves on the wrong end of some bruising encounters. Their skill was undoubted, and they would often notch up four or five goals a game; unfortunately, the defence was conceding roughly five or six.

It was a flaw that frustrated Drake. As a player he had been a prolific striker, noted, like his protégé Greaves, for his flair in front of goal, once scoring seven goals in one match. As a coach, his attitude towards goalscoring changed completely. In Drake's mind Greaves and the other forwards were the first line of defence, and he would become angry when his strikers gave away possession. Greaves, meanwhile, felt the criticism of the front runners was unfair and became disillusioned. Although he got on well with Drake and had the utmost respect for him as a coach, he was becoming riled by the apparent reluctance to criticise the back four. More worryingly for the team was Drake's increasing absence from the training ground. His involvement in the playing side had been hampered by a back complaint picked up during his career as a player which limited him to the office on practice days. Trainer Jack Oxberry was left to coordinate sessions and implement the ideas created by Drake, but often the real essence of an idea would be lost in the translation, and the schemes devised by Drake would become confusing for the players when Oxberry passed them on.

As Chelsea's attitude slackened, so did Greaves, and he found himself joining the flow and taking a more laid-back attitude to his match-day preparations. Terry Venables recalled one particular incident which indicates well the slip in standards that resulted. At the time Venables was in the process of breaking into the first team, and he would get a lift with Greaves to training and to home games.

Jim was the proud owner of a pale blue Poplar, and picked me up at twelve, telling me we were going via his favourite pre-match lunching spot, the Dinner Gong at Gants Hill.

'What are you having, Terry?' asked Jim.

'I think I'll have a piece of grilled chicken breast,' I said, maintaining my stringent pre-match routine.

'Damn good idea,' said Jim. 'I'll have soup, roast beef and Yorkshire pudding.'

While I nibbled daintily on my morsel of chicken, Jim disappeared behind a mound of roast beef, Yorkshire pudding, carrots, peas, cauliflower, three roast potatoes and three huge boiled potatoes.

'You're never going to eat all that, are you?' I asked. 'We kick off in two and a half hours.'

'Just watch me,' said Greavsie, returning to his plate.

Half an hour later we were on our way to Stamford Bridge, with Jim wiping the last traces of his dessert – steamed pudding and custard – from his chin. I gazed at him in disbelief. Was this any way for a professional sportsman to carry on? Evidently it was. We won 6–1 that afternoon and Jim scored five of the goals.

Only a few months into the 1960/61 season, Greaves had realised once and for all that he and Chelsea were on different wavelengths. He wanted to become a world-class player and win trophies at club and international level, and to do that he would have to move to a side with ambition. It was clear Chelsea were quite content to plod along in no-man's-land, picking up results here and there while occasionally enjoying a good cup run, but that wasn't enough for Greaves. 'I feared that if I stayed in the Chelsea atmosphere too long I might lose my fine cutting edge as a player,' he recalled. 'I had talent and I knew it, but if talent is going to become achievement it has got to be properly channelled. That was what was wrong at Chelsea.

Something had gone wrong with the channelling system.' How good a player could he become if he was surrounded by others who couldn't care less whether they won or lost? And why was the club so reluctant to develop him as a player? Enough was enough, and in November 1960 Greaves decided it was time to quit Stamford Bridge.

Football wasn't the only factor in his decision to leave Chelsea. He and Irene had now started a family of their own, with the birth of a baby girl. He knew the wages he was earning at Chelsea weren't enough to provide for a wife and child, and although the maximum wage was still enforced in English football and the pay at most clubs was as poor, he was aware of the bonus schemes provided by some clubs and knew the extra cash would be vital. '[Money's] important to me, and I don't try to pretend otherwise. I am a footballer because I love football. I am a professional because I want to earn as good a living as I can.'

Chelsea didn't share Greaves' ambitious view. The player requested a meeting with the board of directors to discuss his decision to quit the club. The board agreed, and Greaves found himself facing a committee of seven who proceeded to question his plans for the future.

'Why?' asked chairman Joe Mears.

Greaves explained that at twenty years of age he wanted to move forward and felt he'd achieved all he could at Stamford Bridge. He argued that if he stayed at Chelsea he would move backwards rather than forwards, and the only way for him to develop further as a player would be to move to another club. The directors seemed to accept this view, but they felt their prize asset was making a wrong-headed decision. It was agreed that the board should discuss the matter further and brief Greaves on the outcome as soon as possible.

He didn't have to wait long. A week later, Mears took him to one side and informed him of a possible move to Italy. Greaves was shocked. Italian football had embargoed the transfer of foreign players to their teams, but apparently the Italian FA were working to reach some sort of compromise with the clubs. It was rumoured the Italians would soon be snapping up the best foreign players for their league. What's more, there was no maximum wage in Italy and Greaves would be able to pick up in a week what it would have taken him months to earn in England. He knew instinctively it would be the most profitable move for him to make.

Mears told him he would have to stay on until the end of the season and then move to the Continent, to a so far unnamed club which was chasing Greaves' signature. Greaves was convinced he was making the right decision. Sadly, other members of the club were not so enthusiastic. While his fellow players were genuinely pleased for him, certain members of the backroom staff became hostile and uncooperative. Moreover, certain areas of the ground through which Greaves had wandered as a trainee and player were suddenly out of bounds. Irene was even asked to leave the stand where she was waiting for her husband after a home game. She had always met him there without any complaint before; it was only after the news of the proposed move to Italy broke that she found her presence unwelcome.

While the petty sniping annoyed Greaves, Chelsea's parting shot infuriated him and, indeed, adversely influenced his international career. After his last League game for the club (for which he was made captain and scored four goals before being carried shoulder-high from the pitch by the Chelsea fans) against Nottingham Forest on 28 April 1961, Greaves was told he would be required for the club's close-season tour of Israel. As far as Greaves was concerned he was no longer a Chelsea player, but the club had other ideas. It was a game too many for Greaves, and he had grave reservations about ever playing for Chelsea again. He loved the Chelsea fans and sympathised with their frustration at the club's underachievement in recent years, but he'd already said farewell to them with his four goals against Forest at Stamford Bridge and didn't fancy being taken out for another goodbye show. In addition to that, his name was on the list for a three-match trip to Europe with England. One trip abroad in the close season was more than enough.

So Greaves refused to join the team on their trip to Israel, angering the club and the board. But despite their obvious annoyance at his non-appearance, Greaves didn't expect such a harsh reaction from the club. By way of punishment, Chelsea enforced a fourteen-day ban on Greaves, preventing him from taking part in any competitive football for the duration. As a result, he missed the England match on 10 May against Mexico at Wembley (where he could reasonably have been expected to increase his goal tally, as England won 8–0).

Greaves felt betrayed. Here was a club he had served loyally as a player, which was making a large cash sum out of his transfer to Italy, and they were slapping a ban on him by way of a parting shot. It was too petty. Greaves couldn't comprehend it. It's a decision that still angers him. But despite the negative atmosphere he'd left behind at Stamford Bridge, Greaves' career was about to take a dramatic twist.

His proposed move to the Continent had gathered momentum over the past few months, thanks to the hard work and perseverance of chairman Joe Mears, and soon Greaves would be on a plane to Italy. An £80,000 fee had been accepted by Chelsea for his services. The striker from Dagenham was on his way to AC Milan.

5 Sale of the Century

Money was the only motive. I wanted to play football in Italy like I wanted a hole in the head.

JIMMY GREAVES, 1962

'Italy? At the time it was like someone saying, "Would you like a share in a gold mine?" ' claimed Jimmy Greaves, recalling the moment he heard an Italian club were preparing to whisk him away from Stamford Bridge. The disillusioned 21-year-old striker was looking for a club that could match his own personal ambitions, and AC Milan fitted the bill. But little did Greaves know that after many weeks' negotiations, the dream move to the Continent would be the start of a four-month nightmare that would culminate in a £99,999 move back to London.

But for now, he was moving to Milan. It was a simple compromise. Chelsea were unhappy that their prize asset and a home-grown player might move to another English club, so chairman Joe Mears had suggested the possibility of a move to Italy. It was a move that appealed to Greaves, but Mears swore his player to secrecy before becoming involved in a series of cloak-and-dagger meetings that would involve both the player and an Italian journalist acting as an undercover agent for Milan. What followed was a series of talks that would eventually confuse the player, his agent and club to such an extent that Greaves would try to opt out of the deal.

The early stages of the deal, however, were conducted by none other than Jimmy Thompson. 'Mr Pope' knew that Greaves was unhappy at Chelsea, but how he'd discovered the striker was hoping for a lucrative move to Italy remained a mystery. What was apparent was that the cogs had started moving with the aid of Thompson. The footballing equivalent of Arthur Daley was in his element. Thompson had made an initial approach to Greaves over the phone, insisting he knew someone who could organise a transfer to the Continent. And of course everything had to be kept hush-hush for now. Thompson, at that stage, was no longer a Chelsea representative, and he was concerned the club might find out about his new activities, while the mystery Italian club were keen that no news of their approach to Greaves was leaked until the transfer embargo was lifted on foreign players.

Greaves was told to wait for Thompson's call before any further moves were made. A couple of days later, Greaves sat in the front room of his house, idly looking out of the window, when he saw a car cruise along the road and past the drive very slowly. A foreign-looking man was staring out of the windscreen, peering curiously at the Greaves household as he drove past. Getting out of his chair to see if the man was lost, Greaves was even more confused when the car drove up to the end of the road, turned around, and pulled up outside the house. The stranger got out of the car and peered nervously over his shoulder, before stepping tentatively up the drive. Greaves was convinced this was the associate of Jimmy Thompson, and opened the front door to greet him.

'Hello, can I help you?'

'Yes. I am Roberto Favilla,' he said. 'I am a journalist in Italy. Jimmy Thompson sent me.'

Greaves was surprised. He had pictured Italian football clubs as being some of the most glamorous establishments in the world, employing the richest and most stylish people in football, but the character on his doorstep looked more like a down and out than a representative from a Serie A club. Still, anything involving Jimmy Thompson would naturally involve a certain degree of intrigue and mystery.

He looked at the stranger suspiciously. 'Oh yes? Where is Jimmy?'

Favilla shifted uncomfortably on his feet and nodded towards the other end of the street. There, standing in the shadow of a small tree and wearing his familiar bowler hat, was Thompson, looking from side to side, making sure he wasn't being followed. To Greaves it was an unnecessary, if amusing, way of arranging a meeting and he shouted out to him from across the street.

'It's OK! There's nobody about!'

Thompson made a face as if to indicate any noise could alert the countless journalists and agents who would undoubtedly have followed his trail to Greaves, before running towards the house, stopping at the occasional lamppost or tree to make sure he was alone. Once inside the house, Thompson revealed the plans for Greaves' move to Italy. Yes, a club from Serie A was interested in Greaves, but they still would not reveal their identity. Nevertheless, the mystery club was confident that Chelsea would release Greaves for the money they had in mind. Greaves was hugely excited by the developments. The fact that an Italian club was genuinely interested was great news, the suspense thoroughly entertaining. Still, nothing was definite yet and he would have to wait for another visit from Favilla and Thompson before he could mention the news to anyone.

Sadly for Greaves, events were about to take a turn for the worse. The news of his transfer request from Chelsea was leaked to the national press and the country's sports writers were hysterically speculating about the reasons for his discontent and the possible clubs chasing his signature. Chelsea, meanwhile, were furious, believing that Greaves had leaked the news to a journalist in order to speed up the transfer process and alert any interested parties as to his availability. The truth of the matter was that Greaves had informed nobody about anything; he knew that any slip of the

tongue could jeopardise the deal and ruin any opportunity of his making a money-spinning move abroad.
Spilling the beans to a journalist was the last thing on
his mind.

> My Italian journalist friend reappeared. He was more
> certain this time. He had received the nod from Italy
> that the removal of the ban was 100 per cent certain
> now and it could come pretty soon. He wanted to get
> things moving so that I could sign as soon as it came
> off. I said that was OK by me as long as Chelsea
> agreed, but I wasn't clear how much Chelsea then
> knew about the deal. I fancy it wasn't much. At least
> he mentioned the club's name this time: Milan. After
> that chat he called on Chelsea and the two must have
> agreed I was ripe for export because the next thing I
> knew I was called for a medical.

It was the common way of doing business in Italy at the
time, but for Greaves it was an unusual set-up. Whatever happened, though, he was determined to be
involved in all financial discussions, with or without
Chelsea. After another unofficial meeting with Favilla in
an Italian restaurant in London's Soho, Greaves decided
the deal should be played straight with both clubs.

An Italian hospital in London was chosen for the
medical, and Greaves underwent vigorous testing.
Blood, urine, eyesight, reactions – everything was
examined, and a series of X-rays was taken in order to
have a good look at every bone in his body. What these
tests revealed was a knot of bones in his back; several
of them had been damaged at an early age and had
interlocked. This was worrying news for the Italians.
There was no way they were going to spend a small
fortune on a player who could be crippled by a fall or
a mistimed tackle. They began to mutter about pulling
out of the deal.

Greaves was also worried. He was only a young man
at the peak of his career. What if he was to fall

awkwardly during a game and break his back? He had visions of spending the rest of his life on his back in bed or in a wheelchair, unable to provide for his family. It terrified him. A second medical was arranged a couple of days later, this time at a Harley Street specialist, but Greaves endured a few sleepless nights before this next check-up.

He needn't have worried. The news from Harley Street was good: a second batch of X-rays had revealed the damaged bones in his back to be nothing more than a natural growth that affects millions of people every year without having any negative side-effects. There was nothing for Greaves or the Italians to be concerned about. Greaves was fighting fit, and as a result the transfer engine stepped up another gear.

AC Milan's manager, Giuseppe Vani, entered into the transfer negotiations. A contract was quickly drawn up as Milan, determined to secure Greaves' services for the start of the 1961/62 season, tried to complete the formalities. A fee of £80,000 was agreed between the two clubs, Greaves himself to receive a £10,000 signing-on fee simply for pledging his name to Milan. It seems like a tiny fee now, but at the time, when players were earning less than £20 per week, it was a phenomenal amount of money. It was also agreed that Greaves would receive around £5,000 a year in wages alone. It was the perfect deal for Greaves and his wife, both of whom were aware of the short-term earning power of a professional footballer. This would be the quickest route to long-term financial security, even if it did mean moving to another country. Greaves signed the contract, but it was a decision he would regret almost immediately.

These were revolutionary times for English football. Jimmy Hill was in the process of changing the face of English football for ever by helping to abolish the maximum wage and prevent a player strike, just as Greaves was making his switch to AC Milan. It was a remarkable change that was to upset Greaves' plans.

His prime motivation for moving to Italy was financial security for his wife and children, and now it seemed obvious this could be achieved at home. It was a difficult time for the Greaves family, in more ways than one: two weeks before the transfer to Italy was completed, Greaves' four-month-old son, Jimmy Junior, had died in his sleep. He and Irene were devastated. At the time it seemed the last thing they wanted or needed was an unsettling move abroad, but Milan was viewed by many of their friends as the perfect opportunity for the couple to make a fresh start. The cloak-and-dagger nature of the transfer, however, was beginning to take its toll at this emotionally fraught time, as were details of the revolutionary pay changes taking place in English football: the £20 per week pay limit was removed, and players were beginning to earn around £100 per week. In the light of the new sums to be made in domestic football, Greaves realised that he had made the wrong decision and began to regret his imminent move abroad.

The sensational news of the abolishment of the maximum wage was all over the newspapers. Peter Lorenzo in the *Daily Herald* wrote:

> Soccer stars will be able to earn star money next season . . . The Football League decided yesterday to scrap the maximum wage at the end of this season – two years earlier than their original proposal. How much will top players earn? For some, £100 per week is a possibility. Fulham chairman Tommy Trinder told me two months ago: 'I would like to pay Johnny Haynes £100 a week . . . He's worth it to us.'
>
> Footballers were jubilant with the news last night. Jimmy McIlroy, Burnley's Irish international, said: 'Now we have a great chance of matching the continentals and the rest of the world on their own cash terms.' The wages decision was announced after a meeting of First and Second Division club chairmen in London. Now the soccer strike, due to start on Saturday week, is certain to be called off.

One footballer who wasn't jubilant at the news, of course, was Jimmy Greaves. 'I had only got involved with Milan for mercenary reasons,' he said later. 'I had allowed myself to become seduced by the promise of sudden wealth.' Greaves' regret wasn't helped by the news that Chelsea were now willing to pay him £100 per week to stay at the club. He'd taken a phone call from a mystery representative from Stamford Bridge, who'd asked him how he would feel if the club could match the money offered by Milan. He'd told them he would love to stay, and a couple of days later he'd received another call, this time from Joe Mears. Mears had offered his player the aforementioned £100 per week to stay. Pushing his luck, Greaves had asked if there was any way the club could move him into a larger house – Irene was expecting another child and they needed to move into a bigger property. Mears had agreed. The two of them now set about trying to get Greaves out of the Milan deal.

Chelsea were confident they could get out of their side of the bargain if Greaves could swing the cancellation from his side. Of course, Chelsea would have to hand back the £10,000 already paid to them by Milan as part of the deal, and Greaves would lose his signing-on fee, but it seemed a small sacrifice to make. Joe Mears was so convinced Greaves would remain a Chelsea player that he offered to allow him to move to another English club at the end of his first season back if he still felt the team didn't match his own personal ambitions. Both parties decided the best tactic would be to appeal to the better nature of the Italians, claiming that Greaves had decided too hastily and would not be suited to Italian football and the cultural changes a move abroad would involve. Taking the contract to a local solicitor, the club quickly discovered an appeal to Milan's sensitive side would indeed be the only option. The agreement was watertight; there was no way out of the deal without incurring the wrath of the Italians and FIFA.

Greaves was devastated by the news. It was a traumatic time for him, following the recent bereavement, and the Greaves family were under a lot of pressure. The last thing they needed was a protracted legal dispute. He quickly enlisted the help of those around him in order to get out of the deal. The then England manager, Walter Winterbottom, adviser Bagenal Harvey and player representative Jimmy Hill (another client of Harvey) all rallied to help Greaves, with limited success. Winterbottom was particularly concerned that a career abroad could affect Greaves' game and international prospects, but Milan soon got wind of their new acquisition's intentions and threatened to impose a life ban from football on the player unless he fulfilled his contract.

The four had a crisis meeting at Harvey's home in Surrey on 11 May, to thrash out a way of getting out of the deal, keeping Milan happy at the same time. All of them agreed that Greaves had to get out of the move, otherwise the player and English football would suffer as a result. As the meeting drew to a close, the doorbell rang. Harvey's wife answered the door to two journalists standing in the rain.

'We believe there's some sort of meeting going on,' said one. 'Can we come in?'

Mrs Harvey stalled them, aware of the importance and secrecy of the meeting indoors, while her husband and Greaves set about concealing the evidence. Jumping out of the back window and into the garden, Greaves and Winterbottom hid there, sheltering from the pouring rain under a tree. Bagenal and Hill busied themselves by removing all trace of their having been four men in attendance by hiding cups and plates; they had merely been discussing the forthcoming memoirs of Johnny Haynes. The reporters, desperate for a story, began to take notes as Greaves and Winterbottom sneaked back into the house via another window, tiptoed through to the front door and left.

Later that afternoon, Greaves informed his solicitor to do anything possible to nullify the contract, but it was clear that legally he didn't have a leg to stand on. They would have to rely on the Italians' sense of mercy. Greaves was due to fly to Italy with the England squad for a friendly on 24 May, so it was decided this would be an ideal opportunity to meet the Milan representatives face to face. No official meeting was arranged; instead, Mears (as an England selector who would be travelling with the party anyway) and Greaves' lawyer, R.I. Lewis, would look for the Milan directors when they arrived in Rome. All three of them would then appeal to their better natures to allow Greaves to stay at home.

The match went well, England winning 3–2 and Greaves getting the winning goal, but rather than making his stay in Italy with the England team a pleasant one, it was to complicate the situation even further. Having seen him score the match winner, Milan were even happier with their new acquisition. Prising him away would be almost impossible now, as Mears was to discover. Greaves' agent, Bagenal Harvey, was also at the game, but for recreational purposes. He had never seen a game of football abroad before and fancied a holiday; the last thing he wanted to do was contact any of the players, least of all Greaves. Still, Stanley Rous of the FA, Joe Mears and Joe Richards of the Football League were told of his presence at the game and they invited him over to the team hotel to discuss the contractual mess they found themselves in.

So far, finding the Italian directors had proved difficult. Nobody in the city was aware of their where-abouts until it was discovered that a few of the Milan board were staying in the Hotel Excelsior. Greaves and Lewis sped over there with the intention of moving the transfer cancellation along quickly. The initial meeting didn't go too well, and after a long discussion the club informed Lewis that they weren't prepared to let go and any move to pull out of the deal would result in an angry letter to FIFA. Another meeting was arranged for the following day, and for this Greaves decided to employ the cavalry.

Rous, Lewis, Bagenal, Mears and Richards were all in attendance as Greaves greeted Signor Sparachini, one of the Milan directors. Alongside him was Roberto Favilla, the Italian 'journalist' who, along with Jimmy Thompson, had instigated the deal. Favilla looked nervous, probably owing to the presence of so many high-ranking people, but more likely because of Sparachini, who was an intimidating character.

Bagenal opened the meeting, claiming that Greaves had been naive. He was only young, after all, and had let the lire influence his decision. Mentally he was too immature to make a move abroad and wouldn't be suited to the defensive nature of Italian football. If Milan were to force the deal through, they'd be spending a lot of money on a player who would be unhappy. Would they feel comfortable buying an unhappy player?

Sparachini was furious, pacing around the room, waving his arms while shouting at the quaking Favilla. Then he turned to Greaves.

'Do you want to play in Italy?' he said.

Greaves shook his head. 'No. I feel I have made a mistake and I want to play for Chelsea.'

Sparachini glared at him angrily and stormed out of the hotel without saying another word. The party returned to the team hotel, where Greaves informed the waiting journalists, who had got wind of an impending story, that he wanted to stay in England. The English negotiators were convinced they had won the battle. In order for the transfer to be concluded, the deal would have to have the full backing and authorisation of the FA, who were unwilling to sanction any deal if the player involved was unhappy. The Italians had lost out. Or so it seemed.

A few days after his return to England, Greaves was contacted by a courier from Italy who was carrying news of an improved offer from Milan. According to the courier, it would be impossible for Chelsea to match Milan's latest deal. Greaves was about to experience a sudden change of heart. Flying to Milan under a false name with Lewis, Greaves was hit with an offer he couldn't refuse. Despite the FA's reluctance to allow the deal, there was no way out for Greaves. Any refusal to play for Milan would be a breach of contract and would result in a FIFA ban. It was a case of play for Milan or never play again. There was literally no way out.

Playing on Greaves' greatest weakness, Milan decided to sweeten the pill with the promise of an increased payout once the player arrived in Italy. A new contract was drawn up which guaranteed Greaves £15,000 as soon as his pen top had been screwed back on. He was hooked, and in June Greaves signed his second contract, receiving £4,000 immediately with the promise of the remaining £11,000 upon his move to Milan. Until that point he was to remain a Chelsea player.

This sudden about-turn was a dramatic loss of face for Greaves, who had enlisted the help of some of the most respected people in English football. He had certainly changed his mind, but still he knew he was making a terrible mistake by signing another contract with Milan. Sure it was a wonderful financial package, but he knew Italy was not the place for him. He was to learn how big a mistake it was almost immediately.

6 Half a World Away

*This is negative football gone mad. Each side goes on to
the field, packs down into defence and waits. And they
just wait and wait and wait . . . until one side makes a
mistake that brings a goal.*

JIMMY GREAVES, 1962

Despite the newly signed contract, Greaves' relationship with his new employers was on a bad footing from
the outset. He was due to arrive for duty in Milan on 17
July, but Irene was heavily pregnant with their third
child and he wanted to stay with his wife until the birth.
The club responded by fining Greaves £50 for every day
he was away from Milan after the 17th; Mitzi came into
the world on 6 August, and Greaves finally arrived in
Italy on the 12th.

Almost immediately Greaves met his nemesis for the
next four months: Milan's trainer Nero Rocco. Rocco
had been instructed to bully Greaves into world-class
performances. The club was aware their investment
was loath to play for them and had told Rocco to do
whatever was necessary to ensure that Greaves banged
in the goals on a regular basis. It was a relationship that
was eventually to force Greaves into fleeing the country. 'His job was to get the best out of me for our
employers, AC Milan,' Greaves recalled, 'but I was not
interested and went out of my way to make his life
difficult. If he had been a different sort of bloke, he
might have found a way to melt the ice between us. But
it seemed the only answer was to be as tough and rigid
a disciplinarian as possible. Believe me, that was no
answer.'

Greaves found it hard to settle into the Italian football culture, especially the intense training days during pre-season when the whole team was driven 40 miles into the country outside Milan and locked away in a camp in Galaratte for two weeks. Greaves found the days claustrophobic, especially as Rocco insisted that the entire team spend the whole day together. It was a situation that was difficult to cope with, especially following the traumatic nature of his move abroad and considering his problems overcoming the language barrier.

Rocco did nothing to make life any easier. The Italian was overweight, surly and possessed the mentality of an over-ambitious PE teacher. His attitude was a simple one: get the players to play to the best of their ability by any means necessary. He would patrol the training ground, watching the players run through their exercises, all the while clutching a long stick. If ever a player stepped out of line or failed to perform an exercise to a suitable standard he would be prodded and scolded like an errant schoolboy. As the players exerted themselves in scorching midday temperatures, Rocco would sit in the shade, barking orders as he sipped from an iced drink. For the players, it was like something out of a nightmare.

Things were a little easier back at the club's ground in Milan, but not much:

The training was how I like it, but hardly conducive to producing winning results. We used to have two sessions a day of gentle exercises and jogging about. There was a mass walkabout after breakfast and the rest of the day was spent relaxing together. Always together. We were never allowed outside the hotel unless Rocco was with us, and to add to the frustration, everything was rationed. Rocco used to order my food and then sit opposite me, making sure I ate it. He allowed us only two cigarettes a day, one after lunch and another after dinner. I am only a light smoker, but this attempt at dictating when and how many cigarettes I should have simply made me want them all the more.

Unsurprisingly, it wasn't long before the pair had their first falling out. During his first training session, Greaves was pulled to one side by Rocco. The Italian was obsessed with tidiness and liked his players to have a regimented look about them. He was offended by the new signing's determination to wear his shirt outside his shorts, and Greaves was told to tuck his shirt in like everyone else. Greaves refused, explaining it was how he trained in England, much to the disgust of Rocco, who stormed off muttering something incomprehensible. More upsetting than his determination to grind the club's footballers into the ground was his stubborn attitude. Like everyone else at the club, Rocco was unable to speak English, but while Greaves' team-mates at least made limited attempts to communicate with the new recruit, Rocco did nothing but grunt at him. It was a demoralising situation.

Even more worrying for Greaves was his inability to grasp the basic mechanics of Milan's team play. He would attend the squad meetings in an attempt to grasp the techniques employed by the team during matches, but found himself struggling to understand anything that was being said. Rocco, of course, did nothing to help explain what was going on. The club had not provided a translator for their new striker, and Rocco would only gesticulate to Greaves in a strange form of sign language. It quickly became apparent that Greaves would have to rely on instinct to get it right on the pitch, but at least he could express himself there.

But things were even worse for Greaves on the pitch. He found the regimented nature of the game stifling and the Italians' obsession with defensive football frustrating.

Watching a game between two Continental sides gives me a pain . . . There is no such thing as an open attacking formation. This is the system of winning on the other side's errors. And let's be fair about it – it is probably the most successful and fool-proof system of football that has yet been invented, because you can win matches without taking risks. But as a spectacle it's about as thrilling as watching a man push a wheelbarrow.

At Chelsea, Greaves had been used to high-scoring games with free-flowing football played at a much quicker pace. In Italy he would often find himself starved of service, marked out of matches and touching the ball only a handful of times during a game. Italy was the land of goalless draws, packed midfields and obsessive defending.

> Milan played an 8–3 formation. There were eight men in defence with three forwards. And the other sides did exactly the same thing, so that out of a field of 22 players, 16 were being negative. We played our inside forwards as half-backs, with me on the wing, where I did the winger's and inside forward's job. It's a hopeless position, yet it was to fit into this pattern that they paid £80,000 for me. They reasoned that with my knack of turning odd offerings into goals, I should be able to cash in on any small error.

Another aspect of Italian play that really riled him was the continual play-acting that was as natural to the Italian way as the offside trap, but a totally alien concept to a player who had been taught to ride the knocks and play on, regardless of the stick dished out by the opposition. When Greaves picked up a pass he was surrounded by four markers who would resort to any means necessary to get the ball off him. Any retaliation would result in his opponent falling to the floor in a crumpled heap, writhing around in agony as if he had been struck with a baseball bat. After only a handful of games, Greaves decided he'd had enough of

Italian football, despite the fact that he'd scored on his debut at the San Siro against Botafogo on 7 June 1961.

And it wasn't just Greaves who was beginning to notice the negative effect Italian football was having on his game. Jimmy Hill, who had travelled to Milan to watch Greaves play and offer him some vital moral support, was unnerved by the way in which the striker was bullied during a match against Venice.

> Jimmy didn't get that many touches early on. They were certainly not producing the kind of football expected of them. It wasn't helped when ten or fifteen minutes in, a Venetian player challenged Jimmy and kneed him in the thigh – accidentally, I believe. It caused a dead leg. It's not a major injury but it's very uncomfortable and restricts movement somewhat. It would have been in Jimmy's best interests if he had left the field. Whether it was his decision or not, the trainer's or the manager's, I don't know, but Jimmy stayed on for the whole game, making a negligible contribution.

Despite these experiences, Greaves managed to make an impressive mark on Italian football, scoring nine goals in just fourteen appearances for the club, including one against Inter in the Milan derby. But it was obvious that events off the pitch were taking their toll. Greaves' relationship with Rocco and the club was fast reaching breaking point as the trainer desperately tried to shackle the Englishman to his footballing duties. The Italian was frequently frustrated by Greaves' relaxed attitude to the game and despaired at his determination to enjoy himself away from the training ground. In a desperate attempt to restrict his striker, Rocco began to lock Greaves away to prevent him from going out with his friends and family. After one evening spent on his apartment balcony with his brother-in-law, Tom, Greaves later found the door leading to the balcony boarded up by builders on the instructions of the club.

Greaves was often forced to go to extreme lengths to escape from his hotel and the watchful eyes of club officials. One weekend, Rocco learnt that Greaves was planning to travel to Venice with his wife and Tom. Determined he wouldn't leave the hotel, Rocco pulled up a chair from the restaurant downstairs and sat guard outside Greaves' apartment. Desperate not to be out-done by his nemesis, Greaves and Tom decided to sneak along the balcony ledge in order to get to their car and the waiting Irene. Sadly for the pair of escapees, the ledge stopped at a wall and the drop was too high to risk jumping from it.

Clambering back to the room, Greaves was struck by another idea. If Tom could leave the room and create a diversion, thus dragging Rocco's attention away from Greaves' keyhole, he could make an escape and meet Tom outside. Tom agreed reluctantly. Running into Rocco was the last thing he wanted to do, but he walked downstairs and ordered a couple of drinks from the bar. Convinced they were for Greaves, Rocco came down and caused a scene, trying to prevent Tom from buying them. Greaves, free of his watchman, ran out of the building. On his return Greaves was fined £285 for breaking camp, and he was given a dressing-down by Rocco via a translator for meeting his wife at Milan airport. Italian clubs were particularly strict on their attitudes to sex and the presence of wives at the football club, and found Greaves' relaxed attitude to it all disturbing.

His frustration at the claustrophobic nature of this lifestyle inevitably began to seep into his game, and after only a few months in Italy Greaves was a shadow of his former self, putting in a string of disappointing performances. Milan were now close to losing their patience with him.

If the poor performances on the pitch were beginning to annoy the club, then the attention lavished on Greaves by the media was beginning to cause a major headache both for the player and his employers. In

Italy he was perceived as a superstar who was slowly but surely going off the rails and heading towards self-destruction, and as a result he found himself the subject of intense scrutiny by the Italian national press. An £80,000 investment who refused to settle down and play football, preferring to go out to nightclubs and spend his time in the company of beautiful women. It was a great story for the times.

But nothing could have been further from the truth. Greaves was a happily married family man. The nearest he ever got to womanising was spending an evening in a restaurant with his wife, but even nights in a quiet bar with Irene would cause a major scandal in the papers the following morning. Journalists would print a drink by drink account of the booze consumed by Greaves in a single evening if ever he dared stray out into the town at night. Witnesses would recall in gory detail the state of Greaves as he staggered from their bar. And all this at a time when the Englishman was just a regular drinker, not the infamous alcoholic of his later career.

And if the press didn't pass on the gossip, then the local inhabitants stepped in. Milan had many spies and associates working around the city who were more than happy to inform the club if they spotted a player out and about, even if they were doing nothing worse than walking the dog or spending a quiet afternoon in a café with some friends. On one occasion, Greaves arranged to meet an old friend, Gerry Hitchens, who was plying his trade with Inter Milan, for a quiet beer. Hitchens had known Greaves since school and was aware of the media attention his friend was being exposed to. It was decided they should meet in a bar in a quiet back street so as not to attract anybody's attention, but their privacy was shortlived. Seconds after filling their glasses the barman was in a room in the back of the building, calling the club to inform them of what he had seen.

The situation drove Greaves to despair. It got to the stage where if he was to get out of the house he could only skulk down the streets. Photographers would hang around his house, knock on the door first thing in the morning and take pictures of a half-dressed Greaves answering the door. Inevitably, he would look bleary-eyed and tired after being woken at the crack of dawn. Gleefully, the papers would report him as being in an unfit state, or make out that he was recovering from another night on the tiles.

Rather than support him through this difficult time, AC Milan felt the only way to curb the interest of the press and retain Greaves' enthusiasm would be to fine him at every possible opportunity. Whether it was for a late appearance at training (by three minutes was enough), a poor performance during a match (when six other players had performed just as badly without even so much as a reprimand) or a trip to the airport to pick up his wife (he was once fined £500 when he drove Irene to Venice; he had gone past the city limits and was therefore in breach of club rules), Greaves had a fine slapped on him. Milan president Andrea Rizzoli even threatened to make Greaves a Milan player for the rest of his career unless his attitude and timekeeping improved.

Greaves had lost his freedom. Sadly, it's the moment he pinpoints as the start of his alcohol addiction. The frustration of being unable to communicate with any-one for days on end became too much for him, as did the continual feeling he was being held prisoner. In desperation he turned to the bottle to ease the homesickness and pressure he was feeling. There was no way he could stomach another two and half years in Italy, even if it meant never playing professional football again. He had to go home. 'I valued my freedom as an individual above anything else,' he recalled. 'No amount of money could compensate for the loss of it. All my life I have been a nonconformist and throughout my four months in Milan I battled to retain my liberty and individual freedom. I had hardly been out there five minutes when I realised there was no way it was going to work.'

A series of pleas to English clubs to end his nightmare followed, as did a threat to walk out of the club – all of which, of course, angered his employers. Milan responded by taking his passport away; then the British Consulate intervened in the dispute. Greaves arranged to see Rizzoli. In a brief meeting he told him he never wanted to play for Milan again. He was aware the club could impose a life ban on him, but by now he had lost total interest in the continual bickering and legal disputes. Life as a window cleaner would be far more relaxing! But rather than threaten him, Rizzoli agreed, promising the player that if he was to play well in his next few games, he would make a public announcement to the effect that both player and club realised the Italian adventure was over. Rocco had given up, and the club knew there was little they could do except invite offers for a player they perceived to be nothing more than a spoilt brat.

People at home had also begun to perceive Greaves as a stroppy prima donna. 'People who didn't know me from Adam were analysing me hundreds of miles away, concluding that I was a crazy, mixed-up kid who needed a good, old-fashioned kick up the pants,' Greaves recalled. 'What they didn't know was that I had made myself ill with worry. I had lost weight and was run down.'

Three clubs were interested in signing Greaves: Chelsea, Spurs and Sunday Combination side Lakeside United, who made an audacious £75,000 bid. 'Reports have shown you are not satisfied with his performances,' Lakeside wrote to Milan. 'We believe £75,000 is quite sufficient for a player who isn't up to the mediocre standard of Italian football.' Milan didn't take Lakeside's bid too seriously, preferring to play Chelsea and Spurs off each other to reclaim the maximum amount of money possible. However, both Spurs manager Bill Nicholson and John Battersby, the Chelsea secretary, had other ideas.

Nicholson was desperate to sign the striker. His side had just won the Double, but he felt the team needed strengthening, especially with the forthcoming fixtures in the European Cup to contend with. Spurs should have signed Greaves as a schoolboy anyway, and had missed out; Nicholson was determined they weren't going to miss out a second time.

Nicholson knew the player was keen on signing for Spurs following a chance meeting some months earlier at a football dinner at the Café Royal in Piccadilly, London. Nicholson had bumped into Greaves in the toilet.

'Why didn't you join a better club than Milan?' the Spurs manager had asked. 'You could have come to Tottenham.'

It was a comment designed to break the ice and create a bit of humour, but Greaves' response had been serious: 'I think I will next time.'

It was a strange statement to make. There was certainly no humour attached to it. Nicholson knew at that moment that if Greaves were to be offered a move to White Hart Lane he would jump at the chance. He knew he had to make a move for him, and decided to push his luck.

'I didn't know you were interested,' he'd said before wishing him luck and leaving the room.

A few weeks later, news reached Nicholson that Greaves was far from happy at Milan and the Yorkshire-man, taking the initiative, flew to the Continent to sign the player. It should have been an easy couple of days. Spurs wanted to buy the player, Milan wanted to sell, Greaves wanted to leave Milan and join Tottenham. In theory it should have been a couple of hours' work. Except this was Italian football and the club concerned was AC Milan. Sadly for Nicholson and Greaves, the Italians seemed determined to make life as difficult as possible.

When the Spurs manager arrived at the club he was greeted by the Milan president, the infamous Andrea Rizzoli. They greeted each other politely, before Rizzoli hit Nicholson with a shocking statement: Jimmy

Greaves was not for sale. Nicholson was shocked. He had flown all this way to sign a player he believed was unhappy and up for sale, and now he was being told it was all a big mistake. He was furious.

'Why is he not for sale?' asked Nicholson.

Rizzoli explained that Greaves had not attended training for the past two days and there had been no sign of him at home. Now Nicholson was really angry. He had heard reports in the newspapers at home that Greaves had been misbehaving in Milan, but he thought it had all been gossip. Most of it was rumour, obviously. National reporters had been having a field day, claiming that Greaves was nothing more than a drama queen who didn't want to play football, but wanted to pick up the perks that came with being a professional footballer. It was all nonsense of course, but at the time it looked bad for Greaves. Still, Nicholson had faith in the player, and pushed on regardless.

'This is most unlike Jimmy Greaves,' he replied. 'As far as I'm concerned, I've come all this way to sign him.'

Rizzoli shook his head. He informed Nicholson that Greaves was to be punished for breaking club rules. The severity of that punishment could only be decided by a club tribunal, and until that had taken place no transfer could possibly go ahead. Despite the concern of the club over Greaves' apparent lack of discipline, Rizzoli still enquired as to how much Spurs were prepared to spend on Greaves. It was then that it dawned on Nicholson what type of game Rizzoli was playing. It was highly unlikely that Greaves had skipped training; the Italians simply wanted to gauge how desperate Spurs were for Greaves' signature. Nicholson told Rizzoli it was inappropriate to discuss transfer fees at a time when both of them were unaware of the player's future. Rizzoli became angry at this, but reluctantly agreed to tell Nicholson where he was staying.

The Spurs manager went round to see Greaves immediately, only to find he was out. Sitting in a nearby café, he waited until Greaves came back, popping out occasionally to knock on his front door just to check he hadn't arrived without him realising. When Greaves did finally materialise a couple of hours later, Nicholson was irritated.

'Where the hell have you been?'

Greaves explained he had just got back from training, much to Nicholson's shock. The Spurs manager relayed the Milan version of events, much to Greaves' surprise. It transpired he had been given permission to miss training the previous day in order to take his wife to the airport. He had been late that morning, but only because the club had moved to a new training ground and he had had trouble finding it. Milan had quite evidently twisted the truth.

Nicholson was furious. The Italians had lied to him. Now he wanted to get the deal over and done with as quickly as possible. Determined to get the whole thing pushed through, Nicholson went back to the Italians with the news that he had spoken to Greaves, but the Milan officials were as stubborn as before.

Nicholson flew back to London, but a few days later he received a call from Milan, claiming they wanted to reopen talks. This time Rizzoli was to fly to London. Nicholson met him in the Dorchester Hotel, where the Italian was staying, and transfer negotiations continued, but the Milan president seemed uncomfortable. Nicholson insisted his club would spend £92,500 on Greaves and no more, but Rizzoli felt he was at a disadvantage negotiating with Nicholson because his English wasn't strong. He proposed another meeting, this time with an interpreter.

The following day the Italians seemed just as desperate to stall and started complaining about the money they had spent on Greaves and his family during his stay. Milan desperately wanted to up the fee, but Nicholson wasn't giving in to any such tactics. The meeting was adjourned again, until the following day.

The next morning Nicholson met at the hotel with Simonetta Catazzo, the interpreter who had been working with both parties the previous day. It had been arranged that both she and Rizzoli would be in attendance at this meeting, but the Milan chairman had disappeared. Her words were designed to unsettle Nicholson.

'I've been sent to talk to you because we've received another offer,' she said.

It was a tactic that was to prove futile. Nicholson had been doing his homework throughout the transfer negotiations and knew there was another interested party: Chelsea. He lost no time in telling Catazzo so.

The Italian seemed visibly shocked. 'How do you know?'

Nicholson informed her that he had a lot of experience in the transfer market and one or two contacts had been helping him during the Greaves saga. He then handed her a letter which contained Spurs' final bid, but he knew by this point that talks were never going to get off the ground unless he was dealing with the club directly.

After sending a telegram to Milan, Nicholson was invited to Italy to meet with Rizzoli once again. As soon as the plane landed, Nicholson bumped into Chelsea secretary John Battersby. Battersby looked surprised to see Nicholson; Nicholson had expected to bump into the Chelsea man, but not at the airport. Still, he kept his calm and pretended to be surprised at seeing him. When the Chelsea representative enquired as to why Nicholson was in Milan, the Spurs manager told him he was there to sign Greaves. Battersby told him that too was the reason Chelsea had flown him to the city, but Nicholson was unperturbed.

'It's no use you being here because he's coming to Tottenham Hotspur,' said Nicholson confidently.

Battersby was equally confident. 'I shall be doing my best to make sure he comes to Chelsea.'

Despite Battersby's presence, Nicholson was still certain Greaves would be earning his money at White Hart Lane the following season. He had received some inside knowledge on the limit Chelsea had set on Battersby's bargaining power, and that gave him the upper hand. Chelsea was a rich club, but he knew that Spurs would be able to beat any offer they put to Milan. Both parties had been told to put their offer in an envelope and hand it to a Milan representative, but Nicholson had a plan that could suit both English clubs and annoy Milan. He knew the Italians were getting both clubs to bid in this way in an attempt to raise the money stakes received for Greaves – with blind bids, the temptation is always there to offer more than normal in an attempt to beat all competitors. Nicholson got Battersby to agree that they'd put forward identical bids of £96,500 to Milan. Battersby was shocked that Nicholson was aware of the limit set on his spending, realised immediately that he was at a disadvantage and reluctantly agreed to go ahead with the plan. Nicholson had also informed him that he'd already been in contact with Greaves and the striker was hoping to play for Spurs as quickly as he could. To show goodwill, Nicholson allowed Battersby to speak to Greaves first. The Chelsea secretary quickly realised Nicholson had been telling him the truth.

Greaves had his heart set on White Hart Lane and had been dreaming of playing for the Double-winning side. He knew he would be at home there. What's more, he was concerned that a move to Chelsea would be a backward step. They had lacked ambition when he'd left them earlier that year; what could have changed in a matter of months? Despite the fact that he knew everybody there and would have settled in straight away, Greaves knew that a move back to Stamford Bridge would be a bad career move and would probably affect his game. He had learnt as much as he could in his time there and knew he wouldn't progress any further unless he moved on to a bigger club. Spurs fitted the bill perfectly. 'I really fancied playing for that Tottenham team,' Greaves wrote later. 'The thought of it really excited me. I reckoned I would be playing with the greatest club side in the history of British football.' Such was Greaves' determination to sign for them, he eventually turned down a £120-per-week deal at Chelsea for a mere £60 a week at White Hart Lane.

With Spurs now in the clear to take the player back to England, it was down to Nicholson to smooth things over with Milan. The Italians were furious at the fact that both Chelsea and Spurs had put in identical bids. They strongly suspected both clubs were working in cahoots, but couldn't prove anything. They remained, however, determined to get some more money out of the Londoners. Nicholson moved to finalise the deal.

I was ushered into a room which contained eight other people including Dr Rizzoli, the presidents of the Italian League and FA and two interpreters. Once again the topic of the outlay on the flat and furniture came up. I said that that was irrelevant as Greaves was not taking them to London, but they wanted the extra costs included in the fee.

I commented that it was like a scene from the *Merchant of Venice* with them wanting their pound of flesh. Dr Rizzoli thought it was impertinent of me to bring in Shakespeare. 'You are a very hard negotiator yourself,' he said.

I increased our offer to £98,000 in the hope that that would satisfy everyone and allow Greaves to leave the club in good faith. 'The more this goes on,' I warned, 'the more chance that Greaves will have an article published about it which will not reflect too favourably on your club.' They replied that if he published anything derogatory they would take action in the courts. What I didn't know at the time was that he had already sold his story to a Sunday newspaper.

More words followed. Concerned that the pressure of another high-profile transfer might take its toll on a player who had already suffered enough, Bill Nicholson upped the fee for Greaves to £99,999, so as not to burden his signing with the tag of being the country's first £100,000 player. The Italians gave in and Nicholson had his man.

Greaves left Milan in December 1961 without a penny to account for his time on the Continent. The initial signing-on present of £4,000 had been sucked into legal costs, tax bills and the expense of bringing friends and family over to Italy for support; the secondary payment of £11,000 had never arrived, after Greaves had made it clear he wanted away from the club. All in all it was a costly four months, both financially and psychologically.

'I concede that I made a mistake going to Milan in the first place,' said Greaves after making his move to White Hart Lane. 'They were employing my feet, but I could not give them my heart.'

He was more than pleased to be home.

7 Glory, Glory Tottenham Hotspur

It doesn't matter who scores the goals as long as it's the Spurs.

CLIFF JONES, 1961

When Jimmy Greaves signed for Tottenham Hotspur at the end of 1961, they were the greatest team in the country. In fact, the team the 21-year-old was about to play for was arguably one of the greatest ever to have graced the English football stage. Managed by York-shireman Bill Nicholson, Spurs had just achieved one of the greatest feats in football: the Double. Only two clubs had enjoyed such historic success before, Preston North End in 1889 and Aston Villa in 1897, which made Spurs the first club in the twentieth century to pick up both the League title and the FA Cup in the same season. The club was riding the crest of a wave.

Led on the field by the pragmatic Irishman Danny Blanchflower, Spurs' game was based on attacking football. Blanchflower was a player who understood the importance of entertainment ('the game's about glory, it's about doing things in style'). He was a graceful, creative player who could turn a game with the flick of a boot or an incisive pass. Stylish, yet dogmatic in his leadership, the Spurs captain could dictate games with his authoritative footballing brain. In his midfield partnership with John White (nicknamed 'The Ghost' because of his ability to glide past players and into space without his opponents knowing), Blanchflower formed the engine room of a Tottenham team that managed to break the club's record run of winning performances with eleven straight victories. Blanch-flower's graceful balance and waif-like frame wasn't indicative of his attitude on the pitch – he loved to be in the thick of things, roughing it, influencing the game from the centre of the park, where the effect of his presence was undeniable. In short, he was the ideal player to be feeding Jimmy Greaves. 'His play suits me because he is constantly looking for the thirty-yard through pass down the middle,' Greaves said shortly after joining the north London club. 'That's the pass I like – the one that gives me the chance for a quick dash on goal.'

Greaves knew a lot about Blanchflower already, after being marked by the Spurs captain in his first game as a professional footballer for Chelsea in 1957. He was now relishing the prospect of playing on his side; and he was relieved at not having to come up against wing-half Dave Mackay. Mackay was a tough-tackling player, physically strong both on the ground and in the air. But although his game was based on power, Mackay also had quick feet and the ability to pass the ball accurately from defence.

Regarded by Bill Nicholson as his best ever signing, Mackay was considered by many to be the best defensive player in the country and had earned a reputation as one of the game's hard men. It was a reputation Nicholson wrote about fondly in his autobiography:

Mackay brought many players tumbling to the ground with the ferocity of his tackling, but was scrupulously fair, always going for the ball. There is that famous photograph of him holding Billy Bremner, the Leeds captain, two feet off the ground by the scruff of the neck, with Bremner trying to look innocent and apologetic. Dave had been upset by what he thought was an unfair tackle by the Leeds captain. One of my players, recalling the incident years later, said Dave was so incensed that he butted Bremner and the referee ordered him off. The story went that Dave escaped by saying to the referee: 'If you send me off, then the 60,000 fans here will lynch you!' It sounds like a good tale but it was not my recollection of it. I could never imagine Dave Mackay butting anyone in his life.

Billy Bremner has a similar memory of these events:

Dave says I caught him from the back. Well, if you've ever seen Dave Mackay play there's only one place to catch him and that's from the back. You're certainly not going to go head on with him. Dave must have taken exception to it and grabbed me around the throat and told me exactly what he was going to do to me if he ever got the opportunity in the next thirty or forty minutes of the game. Fortunately for me he never got that opportunity. I never allowed Dave the opportunity. I played anywhere away from Dave for the rest of the game.

If Mackay, Blanchflower and White formed the engine room of the Spurs line-up, the rest of the team was equally capable. Bill Brown was an agile goalkeeper who had earned Spurs many a point during their record-breaking season in 1960/61. Signed from Dundee in 1959, the Scotsman had earned himself a reputation in the Scottish leagues as something of a shot-stopper. It was true. Brown was agile and had the ability and footballing brain to close down attackers very quickly, but it took a while for the Spurs fans to warm to him. It wasn't that Brown was an average keeper, it was that he was following in the footsteps of a long line of excellent players between the sticks at White Hart Lane, most notable among them Ted Ditchburn only a few years earlier.

Spurs fans would always compare their goalkeepers to Ditchburn, who was big and strong and could pluck the ball out of the air with ease whenever necessary. Brown was completely different to Ditchburn. Sure, he was tall, but he was also skinny. He was also, in comparison with Ditchburn and the best around the country, a modestly talented goalkeeper. Balls would be collected and distributed with the minimum amount of fuss. There were no frills to Brown's game; he knew his limitations and played to his strengths. Ditchburn, however, had been an entertainer, diving acrobatically and bravely at the feet of the opposition and making the easiest of saves look elaborate and difficult. The Spurs crowd had worshipped him.

But it didn't take long for the White Hart Lane faithful to warm to Brown. It gradually became apparent he was as entertaining a goalkeeper as Ditchburn, albeit in his own way. Shots would be stopped with every part of his body: arms, hands, feet, legs and head were all used as he dashed from his goal line to close down an attack. He was always sharp in goal, and his anticipation was excellent. It was a strength he worked on in training where he would often play up front (allowing Greaves to go in goal when he trained with Spurs) so he could sharpen up his reflexes.

More importantly for a goalkeeper, Brown remained focused at all times. He would have been forgiven for having the odd lapse in concentration during the 1960/61 season, such was the strength and composure of the players in front of him – he would often spend the ninety minutes with very little to do. But Brown was always one to stay in tune with the game going on in front of him, and he would often come off the pitch at the final whistle looking just as exhausted as the midfield players who had been running the game, despite the fact he had made only one or two saves during the match. Brown was always one to mentally kick every ball during the game to ensure that if he did have a save to make, his mind would be sharp and in tandem with the rest of play.

Brown was a calm, assured player, with faith in his own ability, but his confidence also came from having faith in those in front of him – and Maurice Norman was a man who could inspire such belief. The tall centre-back was one of the outstanding players of the Double year, his 6′ 1″ frame dominating the back four with Dave Mackay marshalling any attackers out of the game with an ease that frustrated the opposition. Norman was a typical centre-half: tall, strong and excellent in the air, and, to complete the package, his reading of the game was spot on. Often crosses or passes were intercepted with ease because Norman had judged correctly where the ball was going to be played. He was rarely caught on the back foot.

Unusually, Norman was very quick for a tall player and he would always beat an opponent over the first 25 yards. His pace was important because he was often exposed at the back and would need to cover ground quickly to pick up the players neglected by Blanchflower in midfield as he foraged forward. But if Norman had one weakness, it was his tackling. He was easily turned, and once an attacker had caught wind of that fact, Norman was often made to look clumsy. When he was turned, he would often catch his opponent, but his leggy stride and scooping tackles often upended the man rather than shepherded the ball away to safety, although he was by no means a dirty player and would always go for the ball rather than the man. Having said that, it was rare for Norman to be caught napping, such were his reflexes and anticipation.

Like Brown, Norman found it difficult to win over the notoriously fickle Spurs crowd when he first signed for the club. His build and inelegant tackling led many people to believe he was a bit of a carthorse, but Norman's cool head allowed him to overcome their criticisms and become the anchor in a rapidly improving Spurs defence during the late 1950s. By the time Spurs were embarking on their Double-winning journey, Norman was at his peak.

Perhaps the most important of all Norman's contributions to the team as a defender was his attacking ability.

Contrary to popular belief, Jack Charlton was not the first centre-back in the British game to go up for corners. The instigator of that tactic was in fact Norman, who would be pushed up into attack to add strength at set pieces while the much smaller Blanchflower dropped back into defence. At first, this switch was only used when Spurs were trailing during a game or attempting to secure a winning goal in the dying seconds of a match, but as Norman's success rate improved, so did the frequency with which he would push forward.

In defence, Mackay and Norman were flanked by full-backs Ron Henry and Peter Baker. Regarded as the best pair of full-backs in the country at that time, Baker and Henry were able to cut out any threats from the flanks while providing Spurs with the option to use them whenever they pushed forward. Both were excellent, creative players as well as being stoppers, and would often give the Londoners extra width when they went on the offensive.

Henry was first spotted playing for Luton by Bill Nicholson's predecessor, Jimmy Anderson. Anderson snapped him up, but despite making his debut in 1955, Henry didn't really earn a regular first-team place until 1959, due to the fact that Welsh international Mel Hopkins had made the left-back spot his own. During that period Henry had had a great deal of trouble winning the attention of Bill Nicholson. It was only after Hopkins picked up a serious injury in 1959 that Henry got his chance – and he was determined not to waste it.

Henry quickly impressed the managerial staff with his thoughtful running and persistence down the flanks and would often be seen covering every blade of grass along the Spurs touchline, such was his desire to be involved in the game. Henry quickly earned a reputation for being a cultured, classy player with the ability to pass a ball as well as make an important tackle. He was drone-like, beavering around for the ball, hassling attackers, picking up loose passes before threading the ball through to Blanchflower in the middle of the park. More importantly, he would often be seen haring up the wing looking for a pass as he overlapped the midfield and moved into attacking positions. Often crosses would come in, not from the Spurs wingers, but from the boot of Henry who had advanced up the pitch. If he wasn't swinging in dangerous crosses with either foot, he would be creating diversions, dragging defenders away from the player on the ball and creating space elsewhere. Spurs' game was based on exploiting space, and Bill Nicholson would always encourage his players to move into dangerous areas whenever the team had possession. Henry suited his game plan perfectly.

Right-back Peter Baker had an excellent schooling at Spurs. He was Alf Ramsey's understudy for three years before the future World Cup-winning England manager retired from playing in 1955. Baker was expected to fill the role with ease, but he found the transition from reserve-team to first-team player a difficult one. His early appearances were frankly appalling, and Baker soon found himself the target of the Tottenham boo boys. He became anxious whenever he received the ball, such was his fear of making a mistake, and as a result his performances suffered. It got to the stage where manager Jimmy Anderson felt he couldn't play Baker, so he brought in Maurice Norman as a right-back. Baker found himself on the sidelines again, but he was determined to win his place back. It didn't take long.

Norman struggled in the right-back position, mainly due to the attacking nature of Danny Blanchflower's game. Blanchflower would often drift up the pitch, seeking out attacking opportunities, leaving his defence exposed; Norman would often find himself dealing with two attackers because his captain hadn't tracked back. Anderson, deciding that Norman would be more useful to the club in the centre-half role, moved him across and reinstated Baker at full-back. It was an inspired decision.

Fired by the fact that he'd won his place back, and realising that nothing could be as bad as the abuse dished out to him by the Spurs crowd last time, Baker played with a new-found confidence. Gone were the nervy performances that epitomised his early game; now a new, assured Baker played his part in the Spurs back four. He was hard but fair and filled the space left by Blanchflower well, mainly due to the fact that he was quick and sharp enough to react to any oncoming players swamping the midfield. Like so many other players in the Double-winning team, Baker was a leader as well. He loved to encourage his team-mates vocally and was often inspirational with his praise of those around him.

While the Spurs defence was strong and quick, the midfield was an intelligent, creative unit that could break down the most resolute of teams, mainly due to the quick thinking and exquisite touch of Blanchflower, but also to the tireless running and skill of John White and Cliff Jones.

Jones was a maverick. His style of play was based on holding up the ball, and such was his talent it would often take three players to get it off him. He was the only player in the Spurs side Bill Nicholson would encourage to hang on to the ball, such was his technique and the damage caused by his mazy runs. However, Jones' 1960/61 season was nearly ruined by an ankle injury, and the winger often found himself watching the game from the sidelines. It was during these spells of enforced absence that Spurs' championship campaign began to stutter; it was only when he returned that the club actually looked like picking up any honours, such was his ability.

Jones was a Welsh international, but good enough to grace any country's team. Quick, strong and skilful, he liked nothing more than to have the ball at his feet and run at defenders. It was every defender's nightmare having Cliff Jones come at them. His turn of pace and quick feet would often leave a marker for dead, and Jones the space to whip a cross into the box or feed a ball through to one of the strikers. But the Welshman's game wasn't based on speed and skill alone, but on strength as well. He was a physically tough character and his build, although slight, would often allow him to shrug off defenders with his shoulders and ride tackles. This allowed him to become a team player as well, rather than a match-winning individual; Jones would often be in the thick of things when teams tried to disrupt Spurs' rhythm with a more aggressive approach.

Dave Mackay was a big admirer of Jones' game.

Cliff is one of the most remarkable fellows in the game. He can switch from one wing to the other without any apparent worry, and his belief that he plays where he is needed is a lesson to both junior and senior players. 'I prefer playing on the left wing,' Cliff said to me, 'but I'm quite happy to play wherever I'm required.'

Jones, as I have noticed so often, does not appear to run over the ground. The lithe Welshman seems to skim the surface as he glides past opponents, often sending a defender the wrong way with a shrug of the shoulders or flick of his foot. He is quite the fastest man off the mark since Stanley Matthews was at his zenith, and while I have seen claims for this title put forward for Continentals, I believe Cliff is easily the speediest man in Europe – if not the world – when in possession of the ball. The power and pace of Jones has proved a nightmare to some of the best backs in the game, for, like other great players, he is a man full of ideas – original ones – which he produces in his efforts to outwit the opposition. Jones' ability to hit the ball freely with both feet is something else which commends him.

Ask most people fortunate enough to have seen Cliff Jones play about his most impressive quality, and they will say one word: bravery. It seems like a cliché to say it now, but Jones was a player who would place his head where most players would be wary of putting their boot. Strangely for a short player, he was outstanding in the air and would often confuse taller opponents with his knack of rising above them to knock a ball away with his head and into the path of a team-mate. His contribution in the 1960/61 season was an important one, setting up countless goals for the Spurs attack and notching up a personal haul of fifteen League goals. Such was his contribution that Juventus would later offer £100,000 for his services, only to be told he was not for sale at any price. Cliff Jones was too valuable a part of the Spurs set-up, and one of the chief providers for Jimmy Greaves the following season. Bill Nicholson hung on to him no matter what offers were waved under his nose.

While Cliff Jones was attracting attention from abroad, it was John White who was turning every head at home. A lot of Spurs' success in dominating the midfield in so many matches was down to White's selfless running and incisive thinking down the right flank. White, like so many others in Spurs' glory side, was a graceful player, an athlete who could break open a defence with a flick of the boot or a simple pass through the channels, and by creating space and time with his vision he allowed his team-mates to come into the game and play to their strengths. Many opponents came off the park after playing Spurs complaining that it seemed as if they'd had an extra man on the pitch – this was down to White's non-stop running and his constant desire to exploit space. In short, he was a Bill Nicholson player through and through, a player who had style and loved to attack, and more importantly a player who loved to give his all for the team.

His energy meant that he would still be running into space and looking for the ball when some of his other team-mates were flagging in the closing stages of the game. His small build (again, like so many others in the

Spurs side) concealed an excellent engine and strong determination. White, like Blanchflower, would dominate a game subtly, often without the opposition knowing about it. Unlike Blanchflower, whose strength came from the way he played the ball, White was more dangerous when he wasn't in possession. It was then that he could create havoc, running into space, pulling a defender one way and allowing a team-mate to move into an open area and cause problems. But he was a concern when he had the ball, too. He would pick up a pass in midfield and, like all great players, seem to have all the time in the world to pick out a team-mate in space and thread a ball through.

White was a player Greaves admired, because he knew the way in which the striker liked to operate. Through White, Greaves was presented with a large proportion of his chances during his first few seasons at White Hart Lane. Sadly, this fruitful partnership was ended abruptly in July 1964 when White was tragically struck dead by a bolt of lightning. It was a terrible loss for football, and he was greatly missed. Spurs fans have always liked crowd-pleasers and White was a man in that mould. His first touch was outstanding; he could bring a ball under control from a seemingly impossible height and direct it effortlessly into the path of a team-mate.

It was his technique that first attracted Nicholson to the Scotsman, but the truth is that White so nearly didn't make it into the Spurs team at all after rejection by both Middlesbrough and Glasgow Rangers as a youth player. Alloa eventually signed up the youngster. Spurs scouts spotted him plying his trade in the Scottish leagues and made a £22,000 bid. It was an excellent investment, as White made his presence felt both on and off the pitch. He was an excellent player to have around the dressing room, often teasing and cajoling players in the build-up to big games to ease their nerves, before taking his confidence out on to the pitch with him for the full 90 minutes.

Alongside White in midfield was Terry Dyson, who at 5' 3" was the smallest man in the team, but his height was no disadvantage to him out on the pitch. Despite his diminutive size and lack of aerial ability, Dyson was never a player to let the opposition bully him off the ball and he loved to be involved in a physical challenge more than anyone else in the team. Often an opponent would try to out-muscle him in the opening minutes of the game in order to gain a psychological advantage, only to find the resolute Dyson coming back at him harder than ever the next time around.

It was a determination that was born from fighting a continual battle to get into the first team. Dyson started as an amateur in 1954 after leaving the Army and soon found himself playing for Spurs' reserve team. After impressing in the second string, he was given a chance to make a name for himself in the first team. Despite playing well, Dyson found the number of opportunities afforded to him limited, and over the next five years he only made a handful of appearances for the Spurs' first eleven.

When Cliff Jones signed in 1959 his position at the club looked even more precarious. Dyson began to feel that a move away from White Hart Lane might be the best option for him, but he stuck it out and became even more determined to win back his place. It wasn't long before he got his chance. Terry Medwin was struggling on the left, so Dyson was brought in to replace him while Cliff Jones was switched to the right flank. It was another inspired move by Nicholson, as Dyson turned in a series of impressive performances. He wasn't the most talented of footballers – he certainly didn't have the skill or vision of John White or Danny Blanchflower – but what he lacked in skill he made up for in passion.

Playing out on the left in midfield, Dyson was given the licence to wander around the park in order to create chances for the forwards. In fact, the last place you could expect to find him was on the left wing, such were his movements around the field. One technique employed by Dyson would be to switch wings with Cliff Jones. Both players could use their left and right feet equally well, and the switch would often confuse their markers long enough for some damage to be done down the wings. Nicholson would also encourage him to push up and assist the strikers, and it was a tactic that worked well: in the 1960/61 season Dyson contributed twelve League goals – not bad for someone who had spent most of his career on the sidelines.

If Spurs were strong at the back and across the middle of the park, then the forward line was positively terrifying. The front two, Bobby Smith and Les Allen, picked up 51 League goals between them that season (28 and 23 respectively) and tortured defenders across the country with a combination of strength and skill.

Bobby Smith, in particular, was an awesome talent. Signed from Chelsea in 1955 for £18,000, Smith was a former team-mate and friend of Greaves, but he found it difficult to settle in at White Hart Lane. Like so many new faces at the north London club, Smith began to hear the voices of discontent after one or two disappointing performances. The Spurs crowd felt he was clumsy and not worthy of wearing the club shirt. Once the jeers started, Smith's confidence was affected and his game worsened.

It was an unfortunate start for a man who was probably most people's idea of the typical English striker: broad, thick-set and very effective in the air. Weighing thirteen stone, Smith never had any difficulty in turning defenders or out-muscling a marker when turning with the ball; indeed, it was a common sight to see a defender bounce away from Smith with just one shrug of his shoulders. He would always out-jump opponents when going in for a cross, but unlike so many centre-forwards with good aerial strength, Smith also had great ability when the ball was on the floor. In fact, his only flaw was his timing. He would often make a run too early and find himself caught out by the offside trap, but overall his qualities were eye-catching, and it wasn't long before his performances began to impress the previously cynical Spurs crowd. A few goals at White Hart Lane helped, of course, and in 1960 Smith made his England debut.

As someone with a reputation for being a physical player, Smith often found himself on the end of some unsavoury tackles, but it was a challenge he never shirked from. Such was his strength, he found he could ride most challenges quite easily, but when he did take a knock he would carry on playing, regardless of the pain he was in. Legend tells of one game when Smith's ankle was so badly swollen he had difficulty pulling his boots on, but he still went out and scored that afternoon.

Smith's partner, Les Allen, was an equally competent striker. Greaves and Allen had also met while the pair were playing for Chelsea, and both had grown up in the Dagenham area. Like Greaves, Les Allen (father of another Spurs legend, Clive, who famously scored 49 goals in the 1986/87 season for Tottenham) was one of Drake's Ducklings and was considered a player of huge potential. Sadly for Allen, Ted Drake didn't see it that way, and after spotting a striker called Johnny Brooks who was on the verge of breaking into the first team at Spurs, he decided to trade in Allen. Bill Nicholson had seen Allen play a few times and liked the youngster's style, so he decided to take a gamble, much to the surprise of several people at the club who saw Allen as a raw talent who might not fulfil his potential, and Brooks as a young player who could really make the grade. Nevertheless, Nicholson was convinced Allen could add something to his Spurs side, and he agreed to the swap.

He was to be proved right. Allen was a sensation, maturing in the Double-winning season and forging a reputation for himself as one of the best young strikers in the country, while Johnny Brooks disappeared from view at Stamford Bridge. Between them, Allen and

Smith were to build up an excellent understanding, both developing that uncanny knack of knowing where the other player was on the park. And Allen had the envious ability of always being in the right place at the right time. He was a poacher, nippy around the box, often waiting to pounce on a loose ball that might have spilled out of the goalkeeper's hands, or to latch on to a knock-down from a Smith header. Like so many others in the Spurs side, Allen was also a team player who, despite his shyness, could express himself on the football pitch and encourage others around him.

As a team, then, Spurs were second to none. In the 1960/61 season they won 31 games out of a possible 42, picking up 66 points along the way and winning the League by a comfortable eight-point margin over Sheffield Wednesday. And while eight points might seem like a fairly close-run race these days, the League then was still awarding only two points for a win and one for a draw, making Spurs' achievement a little more impressive.

And if Tottenham Hotspur were a formidable force on the pitch, off it they were even stronger. Bill Nicholson was one of the shrewdest football brains in the game. As a lover of attacking football, he liked nothing more than to devise new ways of breaking down opposing teams and playing football with style. It was Nicholson who really began to take advantage of set pieces such as throw-ins and corners by creating set moves on the training ground so that these breaks in the game could be exploited. It was a ground-breaking technique that Spurs would use to devastating effect throughout the season. At corner kicks, every player would know where to stand and where to run as soon as the ball was whipped into the box. It was a regimented form of organisation that often baffled the opposition.

It shouldn't have come as a surprise that Bill Nicholson was tactically astute. He had played in the Spurs team of 1951 that won the First Division only a season after being promoted. While that was a major achievement in itself, the style in which it was won, master-minded by Arthur Rowe, was even more impressive. 'Push and run' football involved a player pushing on a pass and then running into space almost immediately to pick up a return pass, and while it's common practice in the modern game, it was a revolutionary change at the time.

Inspired by the tactics of Rowe and realising his playing career was coming to an end, Nicholson moved on to the coaching staff at White Hart Lane. The Yorkshireman had been at the club all his life and desperately wanted to be involved with the team in some way. He was replaced by Danny Blanchflower in the team after the Irishman had been bought from Aston Villa, and Nicholson was appointed head coach, with Jimmy Anderson running the club as manager during Arthur Rowe's illness. Anderson was unhappy at the responsibility he had undertaken and preferred to lead a life away from the pressure of professional football. He decided to step down in 1958, allowing Nicholson to run the club he had played for since he was seventeen years old.

It didn't take long for 'Bill Nick', as he had become affectionately known by the Spurs fans, to make his mark. After a poor first season in which Spurs finished eighteenth in the First Division, the changes in person-nel Nicholson had introduced began to pay off, and in 1960 Spurs ended up in third place behind Wolves and champions Burnley. Things were beginning to look up in north London. By the start of the 1960/61 season, optimism was running high. In fact, so confident was Danny Blanchflower that he told the chairman and any listening press men that he expected Spurs to walk away with the title. His confidence wasn't unfounded; Spurs looked unstoppable for the first few months of the season, and they ended it, of course, by walking away with the League and the FA Cup.

But winning wasn't everything to Nicholson. Like Blanchflower, he believed the game should be played in a certain style. He felt the paying fans should be entertained by football not bored by it, and he would always come away from games feeling despondent if his Spurs side had won in an unconvincing manner, even if silverware had come their way as a result – an attitude best exemplified by that remarkably down-hearted reaction after his side had secured the Double in the 2–0 FA Cup final win against Leicester City. 'The match did not live up to its pre-match publicity,' he said. 'Cup finals rarely do. I believe it is because the players are loath to take chances. They wait that extra split second before releasing the ball and that gives defenders time to intercept or make a tackle. Even experienced players are affected by the tension and do not play as well as they usually do in League matches.' Dave Mackay was surprised at how unenthusiastic his manager seemed after that game. 'I'm sure any other manager in the League would have been delighted to have won the game,' he said. 'But Bill was a bit of a perfectionist and he was disappointed we didn't do it in style. The players were just happy and elated to have done it.'

It was perfectionism that drove Bill Nicholson to Italy to make that one further important signing in his attempt to push Spurs on to greater heights the following season. As the 1961/62 season got underway, he knew his team was capable of winning the League and Cup Double again if draws and luck went their way, but in addition to the domestic trophies Spurs also had the European Cup to focus on. Nicholson was well aware of the toll long cup campaigns can take on players and the number of injuries that can plague a squad. Besides, his team were League champions and FA Cup holders and he didn't want his players to become complacent. A new face or two would liven things up a little bit, worry one or two of the regulars and add a new dimension to his side.

Nicholson knew exactly what he wanted: his side needed a goalscorer. Someone who could come up with

30 goals a season and terrify the life out of defences across Europe. One available player stood out as far as he was concerned, a man desperate to move back to London. Spurs had missed out on him before, and Nicholson wasn't going to let him slip through their fingers again. That's why he was so determined to get Jimmy Greaves into a Tottenham shirt as soon as possible.

8 Back Home

*He was a real predator. As a midfielder I found it a joy
to play with him. We kept it very simple to be honest
with you. We knew that at the end of the season Jim
would have bagged 30 to 35 goals, and that was it.*

CLIFF JONES, 2000

While Jimmy Greaves' return to England was fraught
with controversy, so too were his first few games back
in England. His move from Milan to Spurs after such a
short time on the Continent had raised a few eyebrows
among the officials at the FA. Several were suspicious
that one or two of the parties involved in the transfer
may have received money to sweeten the deal, and an
investigation was set up to get to the bottom of the
financial wrangles in Italy. Until that dispute was
settled, Greaves was unable to kick a ball in competition for Tottenham and had to sweat it out on the
sidelines as the 1961/62 season carried on regardless.

The season was already well under way by the time
Greaves flew home, so he was understandably anxious
to stake his place in the side as quickly as possible. The
tribunal was an unnecessary nuisance, and an ironic
one at that. Greaves had been so unhappy abroad he
would have paid the club money to make a quick
getaway back to England. The fact the FA were convinced he had taken a bribe to join Spurs seemed
absurd. He had returned from Italy without a penny to
show for the work he'd put in over there and Milan had
failed to fulfil the financial package promised when he
signed in the summer.

Both London clubs (Spurs and Chelsea) had made a
point of asking for permission from Milan before

talking to me, so even Perry Mason wouldn't have found a fault in it. In fact, if anybody had stepped out of line it was Milan, who were bound by contract to pay me [£11,000] as soon as I arrived in Italy. That should have been mine long before the trouble started, but somehow they overlooked it.

If the League were going to come down on me at all, it was on the grounds of prestige. I was supposed to have got English football a pretty poor name with my efforts to shake off my three-year contract with Milan. But I reckoned I had an answer to that one too . . . and surely they wouldn't punish me by refusing to let me play football . . .

The public reaction to Greaves' return to English football was mixed. The national press had been giving a blow-by-blow account of the striker's experiences in Italy, especially during the long-winded transfer negotiations between Milan and Tottenham, and among football fans opinion was divided. Many saw Greaves as the prima donna who had travelled abroad with the intention of making a quick buck. When things didn't work out as planned he went off the rails, rebelling against his employers by boozing the evenings away in the company of beautiful women. Like the Italian press, the English newspapers reported on Greaves' behaviour in a reckless way, basically rewriting the Italian headlines every day. That the Milan press were making up stories for fun didn't seem to bother the journalists back home, who were desperate for a story. In short, Greaves had quickly become a figure of attention in a similar way to Paul Gascoigne when he moved from Spurs to Lazio in 1991.

But while one half of the nation saw Greaves as a brat, the remainder were positively ecstatic to have him back. He was still considered one of the greatest entertainers in the English game despite his four-month absence, and thousands were looking forward to seeing him perform again in the First Division, with the Spurs faithful in particular welcoming his return.

Greaves, meanwhile, was concerned. He knew his troubles in Italy had been public news nearly every day and he found the level of public anticipation a little daunting. Even more of a concern was the reaction of his new team-mates. They would also have been reading about his exploits and would have formed an opinion about him. What if they had decided already that he was nothing more than a money-grabbing troublemaker?

His fears were shortlived. In the long run-up to Christmas, and in the week following the record-breaking transfer, Spurs were at home against Leicester, and Bill Nicholson saw this game as the ideal opportunity to introduce his new signing to the rest of the team. Greaves was nervous. What would their reaction be, especially as he had cost the club £99,999 and hadn't even proved himself on the training ground? His fears flew out of the window as soon as he was introduced to the Spurs skipper, Danny Blanchflower. The Irishman was sitting in the dressing room at White Hart Lane, preparing himself for the match, when Nicholson introduced him to Greaves. Realising he would be nervous in the midst of strangers, Blanchflower asked Greaves to sit down, and together they discussed the game ahead. It proved to be the perfect icebreaker. 'In no time at all,' Greaves remembered, 'I had been absorbed into the atmosphere and chat of the pre-match preparation. Everything was so natural and unforced that I even caught myself thinking that I might be playing against Leicester.'

The players, professionals that they were, had known there was no truth in the rumours that had emanated from Milan and had been looking forward to meeting him, as Cliff Jones recalled:

We hadn't really talked about what had gone on before his arrival at the club. We knew that Greavsie was a nice bloke from playing against him before in the League when he was at Chelsea. Some of the other lads had played with him at England level, so there was no malicious gossip going on or anything like that when Bill Nicholson signed him.

When he first arrived from Milan there was a lot of bad press about him. We knew he had his problems in Milan because we had read it in the papers and because he wouldn't have come home had he been happy there, would he? We were surprised that he had actually come to us because he was such a great footballer and a talented striker that he should have done really well in Italy. He did do really well in Italy, but we couldn't believe he would want to come back. When we heard the real reasons we couldn't believe what a horrible time he had had out there.

It didn't take long for him to adjust back to the English way of living and we knew almost immediately that Bill Nicholson had made a top signing. In my opinion he was the best goalscorer there had ever been. We were just delighted that he had joined up with us because we knew he was a great player and would improve the side.

We were surprised at the money Bill Nicholson had spent on him – £99,999 was a lot of money at the time and we couldn't believe it. The value of players wasn't like it is these days and that sort of money seemed really excessive for one player, but Bill knew what he was getting for that sort of money and he didn't seem too bothered, so neither were we.

Despite the warm welcome from the playing staff, Greaves was still painfully aware that he had yet to confront the Spurs fans, but a walk through the ground to his seat in the directors' box dispelled any fears he might have had about returning to England. As they made their way to the seats, Greaves and his wife Irene were mobbed by passing fans. Greaves had never been in a directors' box in his life (it wasn't the done thing at Chelsea, and probably he would have been lynched had he tried it at Milan), so the day was a revelation in more ways than one. The reaction from the Spurs fans made him realise once and for all that he'd made the right decision by moving to White Hart Lane. He shook hands, waved at well-wishers and smiled at people shouting out words of encouragement as he took up his seat to watch his new team in action.

The FA granted Greaves a temporary registration until a hearing the following week, so he was now free to turn his attentions to the real reason for being back in England: the football. His first-team debut wasn't going to be automatic, however; Nicholson decided to pick him for a reserve team game against Plymouth, preferring to ease him into the spirit of things at Spurs rather than throw him in at the deep end. Despite the reception afforded to him at White Hart Lane, Greaves was still worried at the prospect of pulling on the Spurs shirt for the first time. He had cost nearly £100,000 after all, and he knew the eyes of the world would be on him. What if he got off to a bad start? Or, worse still, what if he couldn't get out of the reserves?

It was all very well getting the glad-hand at White Hart Lane, but that was going to be my home ground. How were the people on the away grounds going to react? And these people at Plymouth were going to be the acid test. After all, I don't suppose one in thirty down there had seen me play – all they knew about me was what they read in the newspapers. Whatever attitude they adopted, I could be more or less certain it would be followed by the rest of the country. I didn't want to be loved, but I hoped I was going to be liked.

A crowd of 13,000 turned out at Home Park to watch Greaves' first match – it was a gate the first team would have been proud of, let alone the second string. As expected, a huge media circus descended on the game, with the intention of covering every second of Greaves' first 90 minutes back on English soil. Rumours were floating around that the media had been hiring special excursion buses from London, such was the interest from the press in the capital.

Plymouth Football Club were determined to play up to the spectacle, exploiting their moment in the limelight for all it was worth. Before kick-off chairman Ron Blindell ran out on to the pitch with a microphone, much to the confusion of the fans and the players, who were warming up at the time. Blindell had earned himself something of a reputation as a publicity stuntman and was never one to shirk away from the spotlight; Greaves' return was the perfect opportunity for him to get his name in the papers, and he was determined to make the most of it. Silencing the Plymouth crowd, he turned to the Spurs team and greeted Greaves. 'On behalf of Plymouth Argyle, Devon, Cornwall and last, but not least, the whole of England, I say to you – welcome. We are glad to have you back.' It was a confusing introduction to say the least, and one that took Greaves aback. It certainly wasn't the sort of warm-up he'd been used to at Chelsea or Milan.

Still, Greaves got through the match unscathed, but his mind was very much on the forthcoming League inquiry in Sheffield the following Thursday that would make a decision on permanent registration. During the sleepless nights that followed, he mulled over the possible outcomes of the meeting, trying to tease out the nagging doubts that were there despite his knowing that he'd done nothing wrong during the whole affair. 'On the way up to Sheffield with Mr Nicholson and the chairman of Spurs, Mr Fred Wale,' Greaves recalled, 'I ran through the case in my mind. As far as I could see there was nothing to get bothered about. Certainly Chelsea and Spurs, who had competed for my return to English football, had been immaculate in their handling of their side of the business, although I wasn't so sure how Milan would come out. But that was the Italians' business – and I couldn't see it bothering them.'

Following a brief meeting, the Football League decided that Greaves could play English football again, allowing the player to prepare for his debut against Blackpool at White Hart Lane on 16 December. The relief was immense. Greaves had done enough waiting on the sidelines and was sick of the paperwork and red tape that seemed to be overshadowing his career. He was keen to make a start on the real job in hand, but now he found the nagging doubts had turned into full-blown butterflies, and this in a player who had never been badly affected by big-game fear before.

I'd never really shown signs of nerves, but there were times when I suffered inside. This was one of those occasions. I was really apprehensive and full of doubts. Would I fit in with the team that had only a few months earlier pulled off the Double of League and Cup for the first time this century? That impossible Double had been conquered. Had the Milan mess knocked the edge off my game? Was I going to be a £99,999 failure? These were the doubts I had as I lined up for the kick-off against Blackpool.'

Any nerves he had were quickly erased as Greaves notched up a hat-trick in front of the home fans, dispelling any fears they may have had about their lucrative new signing. The Spurs faithful also got more than a glimpse of the talent that was going to grace their stadium for the next nine years when Greaves met a Dave Mackay throw-in with a beautifully delivered bicycle kick that drove the ball into the back of the net. Nicholson was also relieved. He knew that Greaves possessed ability, but was concerned that the transfer might have put a lot of unwanted pressure on him. Now he could see that the striker would be an excellent addition to a squad looking to reclaim the League title and make their mark on the European Cup.

*   *   *

It didn't take long for Greaves to settle in at Spurs, both on and off the pitch. On it, he was regarded as a match winner, a player who could turn games with his pace and anticipation, and he quickly built up a rapport with the other players in the side. Blanchflower became chief provider, feeding Greaves' runs with precise through-balls that cut defences in half before finding the feet of the new signing. In addition to the three goals scored on his debut that season, Greaves notched up a further 28 in all competitions, despite the fact that he only played in 30 games that season. It was clear that Nicholson had got value for money.

Off the pitch Greaves was also proving invaluable. He was a likeable character who quickly slotted into the team banter and became an excellent morale-booster in the dressing room. It would often be Greaves in the dressing room before a game, cracking jokes and easing nerves with his wit in those tense hours before kick-off. 'He was a very close friend of mine, was Jimmy,' said Cliff Jones. 'In fact we roomed together when we were at Tottenham. He was a smashing character and he was always joking. He was good company.'

It was a valuable role Greaves performed in that 1961/62 season, because with the Double under their belts, the pressure was on for Spurs to win at least one domestic trophy. Fortunately for Tottenham, Greaves was in the mood to achieve, quickly striking up an excellent understanding with his forward partner, Bobby Smith. Smith would use his power to out-muscle physical defenders in an attempt to provide the ammunition for the smaller Greaves. But while he was a tough player who loved a physical challenge, it would be unfair to dismiss Smith as being merely a minder for Greaves. He had the ability to take the ball around defenders himself, and was excellent with his feet when in possession. Together they made up one of the most feared strike partnerships in the First Division and Europe, a point not lost on Cliff Jones.

They were very good pals off the pitch and they took that friendship on to it, and it worked wonders for us. Bobby was an excellent foil for Jim. He was a strong character. He had a very physical personality on the pitch and that offset Jimmy's size and skill very well. Bobby would win everything in the air. Jimmy was one of those players who could adjust to any player he was partnering up front. Because he was such a natural goalscorer, he just knew where to go whoever he was playing with. He could sense how a player – whoever they were and however they played – would react.

The other thing we quickly learnt about Jim was that he was such a great individual. He could make things happen for himself if the game wasn't going our way. He could pick up the ball and take it past players at will sometimes. We just played the ball to him and if we played it into the right area we knew he would get on to it. If he was in a half decent position he would score. It was that simple. We learnt to do that in the first few weeks he was at the club. He would get on the end of everything.

Another thing Jim would do was follow up on the goalkeeper whenever a shot went in, and that was unheard of at the time. It was obvious to me that the goalkeeper was going to save it and I said to Jim in training, 'Why do you keep going up to the goal-keeper? He's always going to save it.' And Jim said to me, 'Cliff, he'll save it nine times out of ten. The one time he drops it, I'm going to be there to put it in the back of the net.' I couldn't understand that because that wasn't my sort of style. But that was Jim, and that was why he was such a successful goalscorer. He was desperate to score goals in anyway he could.

I remember one time Danny Blanchflower was the captain and he was the main part of our team, and we were losing one particular match and Jimmy had dropped back into midfield to help us out. Danny went mad. He looked at Jimmy and said, 'What the bloody hell are you doing here? Bugger off up the other end of the pitch and get us a goal.' We knew that as long as he was hanging around that penalty area he would score. We didn't want to see him defending. Once it was in that area he knew he could nick a result.

Bill Nicholson didn't ask for us to change our style of play to accommodate him. We just played the same way we had always played, but it was with a different striker. Jim fitted into the style of our play, which was a push and run style of passing, and we knew whatever we fed to Jim he would get it. We knew he would fit in and slip into things. He didn't look jaded after coming back from Milan. He was a sharp player anyway and was naturally fit. People said he wasn't the best of trainers and he certainly didn't train the way we did, but it didn't matter because you knew he would come up with the goods on a Saturday.

He revitalised us at that time and everyone sparked off him, but if he hadn't sparked us off Mackay or Danny Blanchflower would have started us off. There were plenty of people who would have kick-started us, it's just that Jimmy did it for us that year.

Bill Nicholson had set his heart on the European Cup that season. Spurs had never competed in the trophy before and the Yorkshireman viewed the team he had at his disposal as being the best in the competition. He knew the quality of the opposition was strong, but he felt that with the right draws they could go all the way. In addition, Spurs were very much in the chase for the League title and were going strong in the FA Cup. It would need Greaves' touch if Spurs were to have success in any of the three competitions. Sadly for Bill Nicholson and Greaves, Spurs were going to come away from the 1961/62 season with the cup that was lowest down on their list of priorities: the FA Cup.

A European trophy was a challenge too far for Tottenham, as a physically demanding League campaign took its toll on the players. Spurs started well, beating Polish side Gornik Zabrze, Feyenoord of Holland and a Czechoslovakian team called Dukla Prague before meeting Benfica of Portugal in the semi-finals. It was to be an important lesson for the Spurs team, who were overturned by the Portuguese through a combination of gamesmanship and physical assault. Benfica were the reigning European club champions and a good side – they went on to retain their title too, beating Real Madrid 5–3 in the final – and should have provided an entertaining challenge for Bill Nicholson's team; instead they were determined to spoil the game with a series of cynical challenges. The game was marred by several controversial refereeing decisions too.

Tottenham tried to play a cagey game in Portugal, drawing the home side in before hitting them on the break, hoping the combination of Smith and Greaves could shock the opposition. Greaves had been ineligible to play in the previous fixtures, and Nicholson was hoping a new addition to the team would upset the Portuguese team's preparations. Sadly, it was to be the visitors who were in for a rude awakening. From the outset, Benfica (who included a young Eusebio among their ranks) made their intentions clear, kicking any Spurs player within spitting distance of the football with no retribution from the referee. They scored three goals in the home leg to Spurs' one, although a Bobby Smith effort had been disallowed by the referee for being offside, despite the fact that the linesman hadn't flagged until the ball had gone into the net.

Still, Nicholson was confident his players could turn the game on its head at White Hart Lane. His confidence proved not to be over-ambitious: Spurs managed to pull two goals back at home and had a Jimmy Greaves goal disallowed – offside again. Unfortunately, Benfica had scored first once again to put them through to the final in Amsterdam. It was a disappointing result for Spurs, who had concentrated all their efforts on the competition, as Cliff Jones recalled: 'We thought we could pull those two goals back at home. All the European goalkeepers were upset by Bobby Smith's presence, but the Benfica goalkeeper wouldn't be intimidated by him. We won 2–1, Jimmy Greaves had another goal disallowed, Dave Mackay hit the bar, and we were unlucky to go out.' 'We had set our hearts on winning the European Cup,' Greaves remembered, 'and I don't think I have felt sadder coming off a football pitch than at the end of that second match with Benfica. But for those two offside verdicts I am positive we would have gone on to take the trophy, because Real Madrid, the other finalists, were on the downhill run after so many years of dominating the tournament.'

With their attentions focused on Europe, the domestic trophies were neglected, and Spurs found themselves relinquishing their cherished First Division title to an Ipswich side managed by Alf Ramsey (later to become Greaves' England manager). Still, there was always the consolatory prize: a place in the 1962 FA Cup final against a Burnley side renowned for playing entertaining football.

It was to be a purists' final, played in an exciting fashion with both teams expressing a desire to attack whenever possible. It was also going to prove an eventful game for Greaves, who predicted while warming up in the dressing room that he would score in the fourth minute. His team-mates looked on in disbelief (not only because of his confidence, but because of his apparent lack of nerves before a Wembley final), but they weren't to be disappointed. After three minutes (OK, a minute early, but still not bad) Greaves was on the scoresheet to put Spurs one up. He'd run on to a Bobby Smith flick-on, turned a defender and struck the ball home on the spin.

I darted through on to Bobby Smith's header and thought I'd got a clear run. But the defenders were quick on the cover. I checked to go left to find a better shooting angle. I couldn't see the goal or

Blacklaw, the goalkeeper, because I cracked the ball on the turn, and I think I hit it as well as any shot I'd taken. I just saw it go in the net as I was falling. But I felt ten feet tall at that moment. There's nothing like scoring in a Cup Final, especially when you finish up winning.

Cliff Jones also remembered Greaves' goal as a special one in a tight game that was a much better spectacle than the 1961 final: 'The game against Burnley was a very good game and Jim played his part in that. He scored the first goal and it was a very entertaining game to watch . . . I can remember Jimmy picked the ball up outside the area and he tried to turn with it, but it looked from where I was standing that it had run away from him. He just turned though and cracked it home. It was a great goal.'

Burnley certainly threatened to spoil the party when Jimmy Robson equalised just after half-time, but their optimism was shortlived. Bobby Smith put the Londoners back into the lead in the 51st minute, then nine minutes from time Blanchflower sealed the win with a penalty. Spurs had won the FA Cup for the second year on the trot and Jimmy Greaves had enjoyed a very successful first season, despite all his troubles.

He had already impressed both fans and team-mates, but both he and Bill Nicholson knew there was much more to come.

9 European Glory

We weren't expected to win . . . probably because no British club had ever won a European trophy before and they were the holders.

While the Tottenham players were reeling from the disappointment of losing to Benfica in the semi-finals of the European Cup, Bill Nicholson was busy making the most of the lessons learnt from their Continental jaunt. Spurs' success in the FA Cup that year meant they were eligible for qualification for the European Cup Winners' Cup in the 1962/63 season. This competition was considered a poor relation to the Champions Cup, but Nicholson was as desperate for glory there as on any other stage. He'd achieved phenomenal domestic success in the past two seasons, but was striving to make Spurs the first British team to achieve a victory abroad. 'Compared to how things had gone for us in the European Cup the year before,' he wrote, 'we had a much less arduous route towards the final. There were just three qualifying rounds (over two legs) and in none of them were we in danger of defeat. Our first opponents were Glasgow Rangers, who had reached the final in 1961.'

Spurs, then, were in confident mood for the arrival of the Scots at White Hart Lane on 31 October 1962. They knew they would be tough opponents, but the Spurs side had great faith in their own ability, mainly due to the arrival of Jimmy Greaves the previous season. Greaves had settled in quickly the previous year, replacing the highly rated Les Allen up front, had scored a bucketful of goals in what amounted to about half a season, and was determined to prove his worth given a full season with the club. The bitterness of losing to Benfica the previous season, with those disallowed goals in the semi-final legs, was hard to take. Greaves wanted success in Europe and knew Spurs were the team to do it with. So did Cliff Jones:

We won the Double in 1961 and I suppose you could say that was the greatest thing we could do as a team ... I felt the team we had in 1962/63 was a better team. That's no disrespect to Les Allen because I thought he was a wonderful player and a great scorer. In the double season he scored twenty-odd goals, which is an excellent tally, but the following season we had Jimmy Greaves who was one of the best goalscorers in the world. Les couldn't get in the side after that.

Things were on course for some sort of success that year. We got very close to the Double in 1962. Ipswich won the League, but they took two points off us at Portman Road and that was the turning point. We felt we were a better side than Ipswich, but we had been chasing the European Cup as well that season and that took it out of us a little bit. Had we won that game against Ipswich I think we'd have gone on to win the League because we weren't very far off them, and we'd have won the Double two years on the trot, which really would have been something. We were unlucky not to do that. We played them in the Charity Shield the following August and we stuffed them 5–1. It proved to us that we were a better side.

That result took us into the season where we won the European Cup Winners' Cup, and by the start of that campaign Jimmy had really settled in. I think he was looking forward to playing a full season with us because he had scored so many goals in half a season, he wanted to see what he could do in a full one ...

Jimmy's attitude to playing the game was based on goals. He would go through a game, not get a touch and then get a toe end on a cross and score and he'd be happy. But if he had played an absolute blinder, been involved in the game all the way through and not scored he'd be disappointed. I couldn't understand that because I was a very different player. If he came away from a game and hadn't scored, he was a very unhappy person. But fortunately that didn't happen very often.

Unfortunately for Greaves, that's exactly what happened at White Hart Lane during the first leg against Rangers. It was a game billed as the clash of Britain's footballing titans, as the top two teams in England and Scotland battled it out for a place in the next round of the tournament. Spurs ran out convincing winners, beating the Scots 5–2 in front of a crowd of 58,859. The goals came from John White (2), Les Allen, Maurice Norman and a Rangers own goal, but despite having a major influence on the game, setting up four of the five goals and running the Rangers' defence ragged, Greaves was unable to get on the scoresheet. 'It was strange afterwards,' recalled Jones. 'Because we were all really happy we'd beaten Rangers, but Jim was a little despondent because he hadn't scored, although he'd easily been man of the match. But I suppose when Spurs scored five in those days, most people would have expected Jim to have got at least two of them.'

Spurs had to wait six weeks for the return leg at Ibrox, allowing them to concentrate on the League assault. The Scottish press had other things on their mind and used the long gap between ties to wind up into a frenzy Rangers fans and players – in fact any Scot with even a passing interest in football. According to the papers, Spurs were easy pickings. They certainly wouldn't travel well, and if the journey hadn't taken the fight out of them by the time they'd reached Ibrox, then the passion of the Rangers fans would. In addition, the

Rangers team had been offered a financial incentive to beat Greaves and co. Whether or not they progressed to the next round was irrelevant; a cash reward of £200 was to be given to each player should Rangers secure a victory. Cliff Jones remembered the effect all this hype had:

> The atmosphere at Ibrox was absolutely incredible. I've never seen anything like it. There were 80,000 people there and the noise was unbelievable – you couldn't hear yourself think. We ran out to Ibrox and it was deafening. It was really intimidating, but Jimmy was as calm as anything before the match, as always. I think he just knew that he was a good goalscorer and had a lot of faith in his own game. That's why he never showed any nerves in the build-up. He always looked calm and assured, even though the Rangers fans were baying for our blood. That's normally enough to put any player off.

During his playing career, Greaves described how he was never one to be affected by nerves. In early interviews when he was with Chelsea, Milan and Spurs, the striker would claim an attack of the butterflies was as rare as a missed open goal. In fact he often trotted out the line that it was his wife Irene who would do all the worrying for both of them. It was only later, in his book *This One's On Me*, in which he tells of his battle against alcohol addiction, that Greaves admitted to being a completely different character from the jokey, laid-back individual geeing up the team in the dressing room before a game.

> At the peak of my career, people used to think I took the game almost casually in my stride without worries or concern. In actual fact I lived on my nerves as a player and deep inside wasn't the confident, assured bloke that I appeared to be on the pitch.

Until you have competed at the highest level of the game you cannot possibly appreciate and understand the pressures and stress that the modern footballer is under ... I didn't used to be frightened on the football pitch. But I was always relieved to get off in one piece, particularly during those mid and late 1960s when the likes of Leeds United were kicking anything that moved.

Well, if Greaves was experiencing a minor bout of stage fright at Ibrox it didn't show, and within five minutes he'd surged through the Rangers defence to put Spurs one up, effectively ending any hopes the Scots had of getting through to the next round. Cliff Jones laughed as he remembered the reaction to Greavsie's opener: 'Rangers and their fans were pumped up for the game and really came at us, but it changed so quickly and in the first five minutes Jimmy scored the opener. Well, you could have heard a pin drop after that ... It was quite eerie, there wasn't a sound apart from a few quiet cheers. After that we didn't let the crowd bother us and settled down quite quickly. We knew we'd beaten them.'

Spurs ran out 3-2 winners on the night, 8-4 on aggregate, thus claiming the unofficial tag of 'Best Team in Britain'. But the second-leg victory wasn't without its price. Rangers, spurred on by the incentive of a £200 bonus should they defeat Bill Nicholson's side, were determined to gain a result and a few extra pounds in their pay packets. They put on a physical performance, injuring Spurs skipper Danny Blanchflower in the process. Bill Nicholson wasn't impressed: 'That injury to Danny Blanchflower cost us his services for twenty-two matches, although he was back playing in the "A" team [the Spurs reserves] four weeks after having a cartilage removed. At his age – 37 – that was a phenomenally quick return to the game. Two de-fenders had sandwiched him and damaged his knee. I wanted him to carry on and finish the match and he did so, playing out the remaining minutes at centre-half. He was a brave player.'

The loss of Blanchflower for three months of course didn't affect Spurs' progression to the next round, where the north Londoners were drawn against Slovan Bratislava of Czechoslovakia. While their skipper's absence was a psychological blow, Jimmy Greaves had a more pressing mental hurdle to overcome: his fear of flying. Like Dennis Bergkamp, Greaves and his teammate Cliff Jones hated travelling by plane, Greaves once famously remarking, 'If God meant us to fly, he would have given us wings . . . and a safety net.' It was a problem Nicholson was sympathetic to, ignoring the fact that Greaves and Jones would sneak into the airport bar for a bit of Dutch courage before a flight. The overland Glasgow Rangers trip had, of course, provided no problems for Greaves, but a trip to Czechoslovakia was an altogether more daunting proposition. Cliff Jones, despite being a bad flyer himself, couldn't help but laugh at Greaves' predicament.

Greavsie hated flying. It was a real problem for him . . . Bill Nicholson would turn a blind eye to us having a drink in the bar to calm our nerves, because he knew it wouldn't get out of hand and it made the travelling easy for us, so it wasn't a problem. Jim would never abuse it, and I must say that it never got out of control. There was no indication Jimmy had a drink problem. I was very surprised when that all came out because there was no sign of it at that time, he was just like the rest of us. He was a character, and I roomed with him. He was great to have around because he was a joker and he liked a laugh and that eased the pressure.

Meanwhile, Nicholson had other pressing concerns. Czechoslovakia was in the grip of a freezing winter and the River Danube, which runs through Bratislava, was frozen over. The cold was something the Spurs side

Greaves looks to escape from the Milan nightmare

bove A moment of relaxation away from the pressures of football

op left Gunning for England: Greaves rises high to challenge the Uruguay oal, May 1964

ottom left A typical Greaves goal: balance, grace and power (December 964)

bove Greavsie's England: challenging Austrian goalkeeper Gernot Fraydl

eft A rare sight as Greavsie exerts himself on the training ground

Now in a West Ham shirt, Greaves wins an aerial duel with Chelsea's John Dempsey, August 1970

would have to adjust to, as well as the long journey, although according to Cliff Jones the stresses and strains of European travel never really presented much of a problem for the squad.

> We weren't one of those clubs that didn't travel well ... [Jimmy] took all the media attention away from us when we were abroad, because wherever he went the cameras would always follow because he was such a good player. They didn't want to know about us, Greavsie was the one they wanted to interview. But he took it in his stride and it never seemed to bother him at all. He could handle it. He had a good style about him and a personality so they would want to talk to him ... We were a professional side who had a job to do and we just got on with it. We quite enjoyed it because we got to see another part of the world and experience another culture. We didn't get to see a lot of the culture because we had to play football obviously, but it was an enjoyable experience. The teams we were playing weren't pushovers, though. We weren't there for a holiday, and Slovan Bratislava were a very strong side.

So strong, in fact, that they managed to secure a victory in the first leg. The weather had taken a turn for the better, bringing in a thaw that saw the frozen pitch transform itself into a mud bath. Tottenham struggled in the wet conditions, losing 2–0 in a physically demanding game, as Cliff Jones recalled:

> Greavsie was playing up front with Bobby Smith, and even those two couldn't break down their defence. They were a very physical side and we didn't cope with them very well, although foreign defenders and goalkeepers usually didn't know how to cope with Bobby Smith. He loved a physical challenge and was allowed to go into the goalkeeper in those days – they weren't protected like they are now. Anyway, the

first cross came in and Bobby was a bit naughty. He bundled him into the back of the net and he was petrified of him from that moment on. But we still couldn't score that night.

For Greaves and Bobby Smith in particular it had indeed been a frustrating night, as the Czecho-slovakians foiled every attempt Spurs had on goal. Greaves wrote later:

Like all of us, Smithy was choked about playing badly and losing to Bratislava. As we came off the pitch he made some sort of 'I'll have you at home' gesture to the centre-half who had been giving him a bit of a rough time. Then he showed a clenched fist to the Slovan keeper, only a little bloke, and was muttering something about 'Londres', which was the nearest he could get to being understood in Slav. Anyway, they must have got the message. I've never seen two blokes go white so quickly.

Jones chuckled as he remembered the intimidating tactics promised by Smith in the return leg at White Hart Lane:

In the second game he did the same thing against the keeper as they both went up for a cross and this time he really clattered him. I think it put him off for the whole game because we scored six that night to go through 6–2 on aggregate. Greavsie got two and I got one, so it was a good night for us. What would happen would be that we'd put the crosses in, Bobby would knock the keeper about and Jimmy would pick up the pieces, and on reflection, it worked quite well.

If Greaves found the second leg against Bratislava an enjoyable experience, the semi-final first-leg tie against OFK Belgrade of Yugoslavia on 21 April 1963 was to be a nightmare. The Yugoslavian side were determined to intimidate Spurs during the first leg in Belgrade and adopted the sort of underhand tactics usually employed by Leeds United at that time. It was an overstated physical presence that was to frustrate Spurs in this match, especially Greaves, who found himself walking away from the game towards an early bath after lashing out at a Belgrade player. He was the first Spurs player to receive a red card since Cecil Poynton was sent off in 1928.

I didn't even have the satisfaction of hitting anybody. John White had given us an early lead against opponents who had obviously got this far simply by stopping everybody else from playing. They were ultra defensive and nasty with it. There were a lot of boots flying around and they were giving us plenty of stick. So Dave Mackay and Smithy started to even things out a little bit and I cannot think of two blokes I would rather have on my side in a rough-house.

It was due to what I merely call Smithy's enthusiasm that I got my marching orders for the one and only time in my life. Going for a ball, his elbow caught one of their centre-halves in the stomach. It really took the wind out of the bloke and he went down on his knees. I stood looking on quite innocently when suddenly this fella jumps up and comes at me like a bull. He wasn't a bad judge, picking on me rather than Smithy, was he? Anyway, he threw a punch and missed and I immediately threw one back – and missed. I was never good at counter punching.

The Hungarian referee spotted Greaves' lunge and decided he had no option but to send him off for violent conduct. As he walked towards the touchline, the Belgrade fans began to throw bottles and other missiles on to the pitch in his direction. 'I could see he was upset,' said Jones, who was sidelined through injury. 'And we were playing in quite a hostile atmosphere so I came on to the pitch and helped him off and walked him to the dressing room. Nobody likes being sent off and he felt he'd let the team down. It was something I knew he wished he hadn't done.' Cecil Poynton (who was the Spurs trainer at that time) handed Greaves the keys to the dressing room on the way. It was an irony that was lost on the players. Greaves was distraught at being the first Spurs player to have been sent off under Bill Nicholson's stewardship.

Spurs ran out 2–1 winners, the second goal coming from Terry Dyson, but the sending-off meant that Greaves would be suspended for the home leg. He was horrified at the thought, having wanted to exact revenge on the Yugoslavians in the only way he knew how: by scoring a hatful of goals. He was to be denied that opportunity, but come the game he sat watching with a sense of smug satisfaction as Spurs swept away their tormentors 3–1, the goals coming from Mackay, Jones and Smith. Spurs were in the European Cup Winners' Cup final for the first time in their history. The game – to be held in Rotterdam – was to be an unforgettable night both for Tottenham and for English football.

The run-up to the final in Rotterdam on 15 May was a traumatic one. Blanchflower, who had struggled through the semi-final second leg against OFK Belgrade on painkillers due to the injury to his knee sustained against Rangers in the first tie, had come under heavy criticism. The Irishman had been deemed too old by certain sectors of the press and was made the scapegoat for Spurs' 5–1 League loss against Manchester City the week before the game. That result couldn't have come at a worse time for Spurs, preparing for arguably the biggest game in their history.

In addition to the criticism of Blanchflower, Nicholson's other rock, Dave Mackay, had picked up an injury to his stomach muscles and was looking doubtful. The debate as to whether or not he should play raged on throughout the week. So important to Spurs was Mackay that Cliff Jones opined the day before the final: 'With

Dave in the team we feel we can beat anyone. He makes things happen. He makes things go. If he doesn't play tomorrow, then the odds will change.'

Mackay was the engine of the Spurs team; without him, they often lost their drive. In Blanchflower they had the brains of the team, but the pain in his knee was a concern for backroom staff and players. The ever-doubtful Bill Nicholson was not optimistic about their chances in Rotterdam, and it was to take a combination of Nicholson's pessimism and Blanchflower's wit and motivational nous to stir Spurs into action. The Irish midfielder, who was now the Tottenham assistant manager following his enforced absence during the season, was to undergo a late fitness test before deciding on whether or not he would play. It was a crucial decision, because by the time Spurs had travelled to Rotterdam it was apparent Mackay would not be fit.

Tony Marchi was drafted into replace Mackay, but in the hours leading up to the game Blanchflower still had his decision to make. 'We both knew it would probably be his last big game,' said Nicholson of his captain. 'And I wanted him to play. When there is doubt about a player's fitness the manager prefers it if the player makes up his own mind. The person who is keen to carry on is going to make a more positive contribution to the team effort than the one who is reluctant to play.' But the captain wasn't sure, and neither was his manager. After the final six-a-side game in training Nicholson decided he should start the game.

'But it's not a simple choice,' he emphasised to his skipper.

'It is,' replied Blanchflower. 'It's either me on one leg, or John Smith [the player who would have replaced him] on two.'

After more debate and a painkilling injection to the knee, it was decided once and for all that Blanchflower should make an appearance. Still, morale was low, as Cliff Jones recalled:

Losing Dave Mackay was a blow, and Danny Blanch-flower was playing on painkillers, so it was a psychological loss. Danny, Mackay, Greavsie and to a certain extent myself were the key players in the side. We were a bit apprehensive at losing Mackay because he was the driver. Danny was the graceful one, he organised things on the pitch, Dave won the tackles, I used to do all the running and Greavsie used to score the goals. So to lose one key player was a big worry to us.

For his part, Nicholson was convinced Spurs were on a hiding to nothing. Atlético Madrid were the cup holders and an impressive side. In his pre-match team talk he was determined to make his team aware of the daunting task ahead. Greaves has never forgotten his words that night: 'Before the kick-off we were all a bit nervous, but we got a damned sight more so when Bill Nicholson began singing the praises of Atlético! He was saying what a super side they were, that the centre-half was a great player, the goalie was unbeatable, the centre-forward was unstoppable and so on until Danny Blanchflower stepped in. The skipper said: "Hang on a minute boss. Can you imagine their team talk?"' Nicholson was taken aback and asked his captain what he was on about. Blanchflower proceeded to talk up the Spurs team, telling his players to forget the skills of the Spaniards and to concentrate on their own strengths. Bill Nicholson had put the fear of God into his team; Danny Blanchflower proceeded to wipe away all the doubts the Yorkshireman had put into their minds.

I knew it was the moment to lift them. It was an awkward time for Nicholson. Nowadays it's called motivation, but all I was doing, as Peter Doherty did for the Irish team, was to introduce some humour, to ease the players' natural anxieties, to bolster their self-belief. If Atlético had one or two expensive players, why, Jimmy Greaves had cost more than their whole team put together! They were worried, too, about bonuses, about the fact that the Madrid players were said to be on an incentive of £1,200 a man. I told them to forget the bloody bonuses and to leave that to me, and of course by the time we went out to play everyone would have played for nothing. That's the only way it can be.

Spurs went out pumped up. The team had been fired by a combination of Nicholson's dourness and Blanch-flower's encouragement, and they went on to give one of their greatest performances ever. Greaves in particular was inspired, playing out of his skin. It was a game he would later describe as the greatest he had ever played in, though his own personal performance was not as exciting as it had been in previous matches. The importance of the result to Greaves lay in the fact that this was a great achievement for the Spurs side – the first British club to win a European trophy.

Spurs started well, with Cliff Jones on the right wing linking up well with Greaves in attack as Spurs piled on the pressure. In fact, it was a move by Jones down the right wing that set up Spurs' and Greaves' first goal of the game, after just fifteen minutes.

I set up Jimmy's first goal. I cut into the right-hand side and put the ball into an area where I knew Jimmy would be lurking. You always knew that if you put a cross into the box, Jimmy would be there or thereabouts, and it was just one of those occasions. It was as simple as that. Bill Nicholson never got us to pick out key players in the box in training, he would get us to practise putting the ball into key areas and Jimmy or Bobby or whoever would have to attack those areas. I used to put the ball towards the penalty spot and I knew Jimmy would be there. And of course that night he popped up to score. It was one–nil. Greaves had scored. Thank you very much.

The confidence began to flow through the Spurs side and they pressed Atlético with wave after wave of attack. It was a game of quick one-touch football as Tottenham threaded their way through the Madrid defence. On the left wing Terry Dyson was torturing the Spanish defenders, and soon, chasing what looked to be a lost cause to the by-line, he surprised the opposition by whipping a ball back into the penalty area to the feet of John White, who fired past the goal-keeper.

Spurs looked to be cruising as half-time approached, 'but it was still a tight game', admitted Jones. 'We could sense that they could get back in it, even when we went two up . . . and then they got a penalty, scored and were fired up. They piled on the pressure for about fifteen minutes and we were on the ropes. I remember thinking that if they got an equaliser we would struggle. Bill Brown really played his part and made a few wonderful saves.'

The turning point came in the second half with a fluke goal from Dyson. Turning the Atlético right-back, Rivilla, the midfielder fired in a cross that somehow flew over the defence towards the goalkeeper, who proceeded to push the ball into his own net. Psychologically it was a death blow to the Spaniards and a huge boost for Spurs, who went on to produce a marvellous display of exhibition football, teasing their opponents before executing them with another two goals – a second from Greavsie and another from Dyson, a 25-yard shot that earned him the honour of man of the match.

As the team paraded around the pitch with the cup, Greaves noticed that Dave Mackay, so often the leader of the team, was somewhat detached from the festivi-ties. Moving away from his celebrating team-mates, he put his arm around the Scotsman. The usually com-posed Mackay, realising the importance of the gesture and the fact that his efforts in the previous rounds had not been forgotten, broke down in tears. It was a show of affection that Greaves would later be on the wrong end of during his lowest career point following the 1966 World Cup final, but for now his only concern was to cheer up a despondent colleague.

Still, Mackay's sadness wasn't going to dampen Greaves' celebrations. Spurs had won the European Cup Winners' Cup for the first time in their history, and in the process had set the standards for every other British club in European competition. It was a wonderful, historic achievement for Greavsie and for everyone in N17.

10 The Death of a Team

Looking back, it was as if the team had died overnight.
JIMMY GREAVES, 1972

Just one year on from Spurs' historic triumph in the European Cup Winners' Cup against Atlético Madrid in Rotterdam, the Super Spurs side of the early 1960s began to break up. And while it was a disintegration that wasn't to affect Greaves personally, it certainly had a dramatic influence on his trophy haul at the club. So far, Greaves had won an FA Cup winner's medal and had helped Spurs become the first British club to pick up a major European trophy. In addition to this modest collection, his goals had also helped steer the club to a European Cup semi-final against Benfica of Portugal. But the next three seasons would prove to be a barren spell for Bill Nicholson and Spurs as they set about rebuilding a team to match the achievements of his 1961 side. Fortunately for Greaves, he was still a major part of Nicholson's plans. Indeed, the manager saw him as the player around which to build his side.

There were three major factors in the demise of the Spurs team. Dave Mackay, for so long considered the heart and soul of Tottenham Hotspur, broke his leg twice – on the first occasion badly – in the space of a year. It was an influential loss. Mackay was a leader both on and off the park and his presence was an undeniable factor in Spurs' recent triumphs. Then, at the close of the 1963/64 season, Spurs captain Danny Blanchflower announced his retirement from professional football following a long struggle with injury. And while it was a decision that didn't surprise those at the club or the supporters, it was a talismanic loss for the team. To lose one leader on the pitch was a big enough blow for Nicholson; to lose two was nothing short of a disaster. Worse than the absence of both Mackay and Blanchflower was the sudden death of inside-forward John White in 1964, tragically killed by lightning. The creative midfielder had been one of Nicholson's most influential players and a crowd favourite. His death was a great loss and the final blow.

In 1961, Spurs were the greatest club side in Europe; three years later they were a shadow of their former selves. Greaves was convinced the major spoke wrenched from the Spurs wheel was the Scotsman Mackay. 'Of course it took over a season for the complete break-up, but somehow we were never the same after Dave had broken his leg in a collision with Noel Cantwell [of Manchester United]. Danny Blanchflower was already on his way out with knee trouble, and at the end of the season John White was tragically struck down by lightning. We had lost the three most vital cogs in the machine.'

Dave Mackay's injury was the worst part of a particularly distressing December evening in 1963. Spurs were defending their European Cup Winners' Cup title and had drawn Manchester United in the first round at Old Trafford. United had won the FA Cup the previous season, beating Leicester City 3–1, and were a competent side, despite having finished nineteenth in the First Division the previous summer. Bill Nicholson was confident he could pull off a decent result. The game started at a frantic pace, and after eight minutes a loose ball was chased by both Mackay and United's Irish defender Noel Cantwell. Mackay went in with typical aggression, but for once emerged the defeated opponent and fell to the floor in a crumpled heap.

It was immediately obvious to those sitting on the Spurs bench that the injury was serious because of the way in which he had fallen to the floor. The Scotsman was never one to make the most of taking a knock and was usually on his feet as soon as possible; this time he remained motionless on the floor. The Spurs medical team's fears were soon confirmed: Mackay had broken his leg in two places and was rushed to hospital. It was the beginning of a miserable evening for Spurs, who lost the tie 4–1 after winning the home leg 2–0. The holders were out of the tournament after only one round.

'Spurs suffered a double blow at Old Trafford on 10 December,' the *Telegraph* reported.

Not only did Manchester United beat them 4–1 to win their European Cup Winners' Cup tie 4–3, but Dave Mackay was carried off to hospital with a broken leg after only eight minutes. The cup holders battled bravely with ten men [no substitutes were allowed at this time] and remained ahead on aggregate until the last thirteen minutes.

It was a night of high emotion, a game of tremendous action played sportingly throughout. Spurs, with a 2–0 lead from White Hart Lane, almost made it three when Smith put his point-blank header straight at Gaskell from Mackay's early cross. This was, in retrospect, the turning point of the tie. For only a minute later, David Herd pulled the all-important goal back for United. David Sadler beat Spurs keeper Brown to a loose ball, crossed it from the by-line, and there was Herd flying in with a diving header.

So, when Mackay was carried off, Spurs' lead had been reduced to just one goal, and soon after the interval Herd scored again to level the scores.

This should have spelt the end for Spurs. But they immediately went on the attack. They broke through on the left with John White, who floated a perfect cross for Jimmy Greaves to score with a rare header. So they were in front again.

They held out until Charlton latched on to a floated Crerand pass and smashed a volley home, and then, with only two minutes remaining, the same player lashed in the winner from another Crerand pass to provide the game with a dramatic climax – but you had to feel sorry for Spurs.

Bill Nicholson, while feeling despondent about the result and the fact that his side had not been able to put up a suitable defence of the trophy they had captured so emphatically the previous year, was more concerned about Mackay.

Mackay was in plaster for sixteen weeks, and when he started doing exercises after the plaster was removed, his left leg was four inches thinner than his right leg. He sat for hours every day lifting a 15lb weight on his foot to strengthen it. No one has ever worked harder to get back to fitness. Tottenham lost 4–1 that night at Old Trafford, but such was Mackay's influence on the side at the time that I was convinced we would not have lost had he not been injured.

It was nearly a year before he was back. On 14 September 1964 he was playing against Shrewsbury Reserves when he was hurt again in a tackle with a player called Peter Colby. X-rays revealed a fracture to the same leg. Apparently the bones had joined together too solidly the first time, affecting his blood circulation. I was with the first team at West Ham when I heard the distressing news. I returned to White Hart Lane and was told Dave had said, 'Bill Nick is going to go mad when he hears about this.'

Many people, including the fans, felt the second blow would be too much of a hurdle to overcome for the tough Scottish international. The national press were equally dismissive of Mackay's chances of a second comeback. 'Spurs and Scotland left-half Dave Mackay has broken his leg again in a comeback match after nine gritty months spent regaining fitness,' wrote the *Telegraph*.

133

Playing for the reserves against Shrewsbury reserves at White Hart Lane on 14 September, he suddenly spun agonisingly to the ground just outside the opposition penalty area, clutching the same leg that he broke against Manchester United in the European Cup Winners' Cup.

There are no stouter hearts in football than the fearless midfield dynamo, inspiration of all his colleagues. But he will need all his courage, only two months from his 30th birthday, to come back again from such a devastating blow.

But of course he did make a comeback, this time avoiding the fatty foods and drink that had put so much weight on him during his previous rehabilitation. The second time around, Mackay returned with the same confidence and composure that had inspired the Spurs team during the previous season. It was almost as if he had never been away. It was obvious that Spurs had struggled in his absence, although Mackay's injury had made little difference to Greaves' performances. What was apparent, however, was that the striker was missing another of the cogs of the Double-winning machine: Danny Blanchflower.

Greaves had been in awe of Blanchflower from the moment he started his career at White Hart Lane, not only because of the Irishman's creative intelligence on the pitch, but because of his incredible presence off it. As a leader and a captain Blanchflower had been second to none, sparing no detail when preparing for a forthcoming match. Team discussions with Bill Nicholson would often turn into The Danny Blanchflower Show, as the Irishman ran through every factor of the game plan from the referee to the colour of the corner flags. Greaves had often sat enthralled by these discussions and Blanchflower's obvious passion for the game. He wrote at the time:

Most of the tactical sessions end up the same way, with Mr Nicholson and Danny having a long involved argument which sounds like a debate between a mathematician and a philosopher. They're similar types – they've both got this fantastic devotion to the game, so they just can't help getting each other going. They give the same consideration to the smallest details as they do the biggest. That's why they rate among the greatest brains in the game in England today. [Danny's] the Commander-in-Chief once we start a match. He gives his orders, sorts out the problems with a serene and unshakeable belief that he is right. On the football pitch (or off it, for that matter) I don't suppose Blanchflower has ever funked an issue in his life.

Greaves and Blanchflower had certainly sparked off each other. In the months leading up to Greaves' arrival at White Hart Lane, Blanchflower had looked jaded, but the striker's arrival had prompted a resurgence in the Irishman. The two players had had an instinctive understanding of each other when they were on the pitch, with Blanchflower often providing the killer pass that could split a defence and release Greaves on goal. 'Jimmy absolutely worshipped Danny,' said Cliff Jones. 'He loved him to bits and thought he was wonderful. He even named his son after him.'

Blanchflower had known his career was coming to a close in the summer of 1962, following the FA Cup victory over Burnley. With one or two members of the Spurs team (Greaves included) heading off for international duty in Chile for the World Cup, Blanchflower had had plenty of time to consider his future. His international career had been finished by a knee injury, and his club career was ultimately to be finished by a similar injury, the one he picked up during the Cup Winners' Cup tie against Rangers in December 1962. 'I was nearing my 37th birthday and feeling I could play until I was 40,' he recalled. 'I liked the big games, they brought the best out of me. I was playing well until I was struck from behind. My knee felt like the twisted strings of a harp.' Blanchflower had just about managed to regain his fitness in time for Spurs' historic win in Europe, but the following season he announced his retirement to the national press.

DANNY BOY BOWS OUT screamed the headline in the *Telegraph*.

Danny Blanchflower, 38, announced he will be retiring from football at the end of the season when his contract with Spurs expires. He was dropped from the first team in November and later aggravated a knee injury playing for the reserves. Last month Bill Nicholson paid Fulham £72,500 for Alan Mullery, a British record for a half-back, to take over from Blanchflower.

Blanchflower, who made his League debut for Barnsley in 1949, cost Spurs a then club record £30,000 when they bought him from Aston Villa in 1954, arguably the best money they ever spent. A constructive right-half, he led them to this century's first League and Cup double in 1961 and to the first British success in Europe last season, when they won the Cup Winners' Cup. He also played the last of his record 56 Irish internationals last season.

A cultured footballer with a cultured mind (which he has never been afraid to speak!), he has not always seen eye to eye with management. But he has been a supreme leader both for club and country, a master tactician, respected and revered by those he has played with.

Greaves persevered in Blanchflower's absence, and his hard work was rewarded. During the Irishman's last season, 1963/64, in which he made very few appearances, Greaves became the League's highest goalscorer for the fourth time in his career with 35 goals to his name, inspiring Spurs to a very creditable fourth place in the First Division. But, as he later admitted, these few years were a very difficult period in his playing career, trying to perform at his peak day in, day out in a side bereft of Mackay, Blanchflower and White. He particularly grew to miss the sharp wing play and probing crosses of the latter.

It hurts me to talk about John White. His death was a terrible blow to Tottenham and the whole of football. John was a great, great player when he died and I am convinced he was going to get even better. He was so aptly named the Ghost of White Hart Lane. It was his ability off the ball that made him such a phenomenal player. He would pop up in the right place from out of nowhere just when he was needed to make a pass or collect a ball and, like Danny Blanchflower and Dave Mackay, he could run all day.

White's body was found under a tree at Crews Hill golf course in London on 21 July 1964. He had been spending the afternoon out on the golf course on his own, as he was wont to do, when a thunderstorm came over. As the rain came down, White decided to shelter under a nearby tree and wait for the storm to pass. In hindsight it was a foolish thing to do. Before long, a bolt of lightning came out of nowhere and struck White through the tree. Had he received medical attention immediately, it might have been possible to start his heart beating; as it was, he was alone, and he died before anyone could get to him.

The football world mourned and news of White's death was carried in all the dailies. 'John White, the Spurs and Scotland inside forward, was struck by lightning and killed while playing golf on 21 July,' wrote the *Telegraph*.

His wife had dropped him at the Crews Hill club, Enfield, and he had just driven off the first tee when it started raining. He took shelter under a line of oak trees, and was seen sitting under one by golfers running for the clubhouse. There was a single flash of lightning, and White's body was later found by two groundsmen.

White's tragic death at 27 is a terrible blow to his family, to Spurs and to football as a whole. His frail physique belied the strength in his legs, and although he was best known for his defence-splitting passes, he also had a fierce shot. He earned the nickname 'Ghost of White Hart Lane' for his uncanny ability to drift unseen into dangerous positions. His midfield partnership with Danny Blanchflower was at the heart of Spurs' 'double' triumph in 1961 and their later successes in domestic and European cups. He won 22 international caps and will be sorely missed by both club and country.

White's wife Sandra was too shocked to identify the body, and the job was handed to Bill Nicholson. Tottenham police made a phone call to the Nicholson household and reported what had happened. The Spurs manager was audibly annoyed. He had already received several prank calls that week regarding Greaves. A joker had been ringing up claiming that the striker had been killed in a car crash, and this just seemed to be another bad-taste joke along similar lines. Nicholson asked the caller to give him his number so that he could call him back; he redialled immediately and found he was through to Tottenham police station, greeted by the same voice that had broken the bad news to him seconds before. Nicholson had lost a great player and a wonderful friend, and he knew once and for all that his Spurs side would never be the same again.

Moreover, a number of other players had for various reasons made their way out of White Hart Lane: Tony Marchi went on to become the manager of Cambridge City; Terry Dyson was transferred to Fulham; Les Allen moved over the city to Queens Park Rangers (he'd always struggled to get into the Spurs side following the signing of Greaves, despite being a formidable striker himself); and Bobby Smith was sold to Brighton in Division Three. Undaunted, Nicholson set about building a new team, with Greaves very much in mind as his first-choice striker. As a replacement for Blanchflower he'd already bought Mullery from Fulham (a role he was to find mentally demanding because of the success of the former Spurs captain and the expectations of the White Hart Lane crowd); the priority now, with Allen and Smith gone, was to find a quality strike partner for Greaves.

After scouring the country, Nicholson settled on Alan Gilzean, who was playing for Dundee and had made a name for himself by scoring a number of goals in his club's run in the European Cup the previous season. Nicholson was impressed with Gilzean. He was a big, strong player who was excellent in the air and equally good with the ball at his feet. With his aerial strength and vision, he would make the perfect foil for Greaves, the League's most prolific striker. But Nicholson had competition: both Sunderland and Italian club Torino were interested in the Scotsman, but a quick conversation with Denis Law (who had been at Torino) dissuaded 'Gilly' from moving to the Continent. Nicholson finally signed his man in December 1964, in the player's car by the River Tay, Gilzean accepting a lower pay offer than the one put on the table by Sunderland. Gilzean cost £72,000, but it was money well spent. Nicholson felt he had a player who could bring the best out of Greaves.

As the manager of a rich club, I knew I had to pay above the market rate for players, and it had the effect of forcing prices up in the transfer market. I regretted that, but I had to do my best to strengthen the side. When a club knew I was interested in one of their players, it would deliberately ask for a higher price.

I liked Gilly. He was easy to talk to, never moaned and got on with the job in an uncomplicated way. He was an unorthodox player, different in many ways from Bobby Smith. He was more of a footballing centre-forward and started his career as an inside left. He didn't head the ball full on like Smith. He preferred to glance it on as he turned his head. It was not a style you could coach in anyone because the margin of error was so small. But it suited him, and I never tried to change him.

Greaves was equally enthusiastic about the employment of Gilzean, and in the remaining months of their first season together, 1964/65, they hit it off almost immediately, forming one of the most lethal partnerships in the First Division, surpassing the strength and skill of the Greaves–Smith combination.

What a difference with Alan Gilzean! We were made for each other. We had an understanding right from the off and I was never happier than when playing with Gilly by my side. I was as comfortable with him as I had been with big Bobby Smith. I don't think Gilly gets nearly enough credit, perhaps because he is a deep Scot who doesn't try to cultivate an image for himself off the pitch. I would say he is one of the greatest players I have ever seen or played with. He is tremendously talented on the ball, is a master of the flick header and is a lot harder and braver than many critics seem to think.

And there were other acquisitions too, all part of Nicholson's grand plan: Pat Jennings from Watford for £30,000; Jimmy Robertson from St Mirren for £25,000; Laurie Brown from Arsenal for £40,000; and Cyril Knowles from Middlesbrough for £45,000. And in May 1966 the squad was strengthened further when Nicholson spent £80,000 on Chelsea's Terry Venables; by the August he'd also signed Mike England from Blackburn for £95,000. It was a spending spree that had spanned some twenty months. The result was a side that would match the style and flair of the Double-winning side (albeit without its phenomenal success) and help secure Jimmy Greaves his last trophy win with the club.

11 Greavsie's England

This young man of the lightning speed, deadly positioning in the penalty area, and fiercely accurate finishing, had been making the news with Chelsea, and he and I found a happy marriage of styles.

JOHNNY HAYNES, 1962

Jimmy Greaves was being tipped for international stardom from the moment he scored on his Chelsea debut at White Hart Lane on 23 August 1957. In fact, so rapid was his rise to prominence that Greaves actually made his England U23 debut after only eight games in a Chelsea shirt. Granted, he had scored six times in a handful of games, but he was still only seventeen and many, including Greaves himself, felt he was too young. The attention didn't bother him, however; he found the praise flattering. The responsibility of representing his country wouldn't add any extra nerves either, it was just that he hadn't anticipated pulling on the white shirt of England at such an early stage.

The U23 team had been the brainchild of senior national manager Walter Winterbottom. Realising that throwing youngsters into a full international game without any relevant experience often produced disappointing performances, the England manager set up a nursery team in which the country's bright young talent could develop, before parading their skills on the world stage. By instituting an U23 set-up he had created a sense of continuity within the broad England set-up and a team spirit between the youngsters and senior players. The team was a success from the start, and had produced potential stars such as Johnny Haynes of

Fulham, who would later go on to be a prolific full international.

Haynes was experienced at both club and international level and would be Greaves' partner at Stamford Bridge for his England U23 debut against Bulgaria, the first international of the season.

I captained the team and with it said a farewell to a golden career in this team. From now on it was to be the senior team or nothing. I led the team on with very mixed emotions. I had been in from the start of these matches, having been reserve for the first one in Bologna, Italy, nearly 30 months earlier, and had never played on a losing side. This class of international football had taken me back to the full England side, kept me in it, and given me invaluable experience of foreign teams, foreign styles and places. And the value of such fixtures was proved that very night when a new star shot across the international sky: Jimmy Greaves of Chelsea.

It was a 'marriage of styles' that was to reap dividends immediately: England destroyed Bulgaria 6–2, Greaves and Haynes grabbing two goals each. The press gushed about Greaves' performances and made noises about blooding him in the full team for a possible squad number in the 1958 World Cup finals in Sweden. 'More than 56,000 people at Stamford Bridge were shown that Johnny Haynes and Jimmy Greaves are natural partners,' wrote the *Star*. 'There has been nothing like this from an England pair since the great days of Raich Carter and Wilf Mannion. Greaves, making his Under-23 international debut, scored twice and missed a penalty during an eventful first match . . .'

The penalty miss didn't bother Greaves. He was delighted to have scored for his country and was excited at the rapport he had struck up with Johnny Haynes. It was a partnership he would later describe as the best in his career, and the two would later reunite at full international level. Greaves enjoyed playing at this level and was determined to keep his place in the U23 side. The striker went from strength to strength, and in the next eleven games scored another eleven goals. By this stage the selectors were convinced he was ready to play for the full team, and in 1959, at the age of nineteen, Jimmy Greaves was invited on the England tour of South America.

The 1958 World Cup had passed him by, despite the media clamour for his inclusion, mainly because he'd hit a barren patch late in 1957 and Ted Drake, deciding it was best to protect his young talent, had rested him. But by the summer of 1959 Greaves was big news and the tour of South America was the perfect international stage on which to parade his skills. The tour, however, was a disaster. England were scheduled to play Brazil, Peru, Mexico and the United States in fifteen days, poor results frustrated everyone, and things gradually descended into a logistical nightmare.

The opening game against Brazil in Rio on 13 May was a poor one, England losing to the world champions 2–0. Greaves watched from the sidelines that day, but he found himself in the starting line-up four days later for the match against Peru. For England it was again a disappointing afternoon, the Peruvians destroying Winterbottom's team by four goals to one. Despite the scoreline, the game was a personal triumph for Greaves, who scored England's only goal. 'Jimmy Greaves, making his international debut for England against Peru in Lima, scored the first of what will surely be many goals for his country,' gushed the *Empire News* the following day. 'His performance was a rare bright spot in a humiliating 4–1 defeat that once again emphasised that drastic changes must be made at the top. Make no mistake, this is crisis time for England.'

Drastic changes could not be made within the week, though, and England lost their third game on the trot in Mexico City. They redeemed themselves a little in their last game of the tour in Los Angeles by humiliating the

Americans 8–1 (bizarrely without Greaves managing to get on the scoresheet), but the national press was already well underway with its witch hunt. Their target was Walter Winterbottom. Many felt that the England manager was not good enough for the job, that the standard of football was not up to scratch (sound familiar?). The campaign against Winterbottom got so venomous that the FA had to issue a statement in the autumn of 1959 denying newspaper rumours insisting that Winterbottom was about to be sacked. It had been a bad season for the England boss, who was desperately trying to experiment with players in order to mould a squad strong enough to win the 1962 World Cup in Chile.

In stark contrast to his manager, Greavsie was enjoying himself. In the first game back on home soil following the South America debacle England drew 1–1 with Wales, Greaves claiming his second international goal. A 3–2 defeat at the hands of Sweden at Wembley followed at the end of October, a poor result Greaves attributed to the loss of Johnny Haynes, as well as poor tactics.

> Johnny Haynes was out through injury, which is just about the worst luck any selector has been capable of experiencing over the past three years [to 1962], and I kept my place. The two inside forwards were Bobby Charlton and myself with Brian Clough in the middle. I can't imagine a more lop-sided combination. We all had the same lop-sided idea – we all wanted to go hell for leather for goal. That was all right as far as Clough was concerned, but with Charlton and myself being players of a similar type, it meant there was no link in midfield between attack and defence. We couldn't have had Haynes, but without another inside forward we were lost.

The side was abandoned after those two disappointing results and Greaves was dropped for a couple of games (against Northern Ireland and Scotland) as

Winterbottom continued with his experimentation. He was recalled against Yugoslavia in May 1960, bagging his third goal for his country, and then went on the England tour of Spain and Hungary. Although the results were again poor (0–3 and 0–2 respectively), the performances were good, and it was becoming apparent that Winterbottom's tinkering with the make-up of the side was paying off. England were starting to gel and the feeling in the camp was that they weren't far short of being a very good side.

In the 1960/61 season the hunch that England were on the verge of great things became a reality when, starting on 8 October in Belfast with a 5–2 drubbing of the home side, Winterbottom's men went eight games without defeat in a year that culminated in a 'suicidal' tour of western Europe – 'suicidal' because it would take in games against Portugal and Austria, then considered to be two of the best teams in international football (Austria was the only defeat, however). During that winning run, Greaves was in excellent form, scoring eleven goals as the partnership with Haynes began to reap dividends. 'Jimmy Greaves is a remarkable young man,' Haynes opined.

> He may well prove to be one of the greatest goal-scorers the world has ever known. No player has ever had such a facility for being in the right place at the right time in the penalty area, no player has ever had such cold finishing power. Greaves is tremendously fast, but deceptively fast. When he is moving with the ball defenders often look like reaching him but in fact they never get close, so smoothly does he accelerate. And when he is in a shooting position, all this hectic speed seems to vanish and everything stops and he has all the time in the world to score. All this is an illusion because of his remarkable balance.

After Belfast, England travelled to Luxembourg for a World Cup qualifier and overwhelmed the national side

9–0, Greaves claiming his first England hat-trick, but the real test would be a week later at Wembley. Spain were the visitors on 26 October for a friendly, with a side that included Di Stefano and several other Real Madrid stars. The Spaniards had earned themselves a reputation as one of the strongest sides in Europe; they were, as Greaves described them, 'the masters'. The crown was to be knocked off their heads under the twin towers, though, Greaves hitting the back of the net once in a thoroughly satisfying 4–2 victory. It was a good indication that Winterbottom and England had learnt the harsh lessons dealt out on the South American tour.

Well, we won 4–2 and the thing was proved. Spain went down, beaten soundly and convincingly, and we were a world-ranking football power again. Wales copped it next, 5–1, and then Scotland, a record 9–3 at Wembley. Now it was time for Portugal in Lisbon in the preliminaries of the World Cup. This is what all the hoping and the struggling had been for. We had to keep Portugal within overhauling distance so that we could qualify for Chile when they played the return at Wembley.

In this vital qualifier in May 1961, England achieved Greaves' wishes by securing a satisfactory 1–1 draw against a side that included eight of the impressive Benfica team, then beat them 2–0 five months later at Wembley. Greaves was unable to play at Wembley owing to a commitment in Italy (he had joined AC Milan by this point), but he knew he was on his way to Chile. Some of the players were concerned that his time away from English football might affect his game, but their concerns were, of course, to be shortlived.

Greaves' game was fine, but it was apparent that the team wasn't functioning as well as it had the previous season as results for 1961/62 were mixed. The 1962 World Cup Finals were a matter of months away and England seemed once again to be struggling to find their feet. Greaves, not to mention his manager, was concerned.

Something went wrong in the 1961/62 season. Something went out of our play just when we needed it to be at its best for there were to be no more chances at reshaping – Chile was only months away. I can't speak of [some] of the games because I didn't play in them [owing to his stay in Italy]. But the results weren't as good as we'd hoped they would be.

I returned after my Italian interlude to the England side to play Scotland at Hampden Park [14 April 1962]. The World Cup was close now, and we were trounced by a fine moving Scots side that made us look shoddy. My contribution to the game was nil. I played as if I came from a long line of odd-men-out. I think Italy messed us up. I think the lure of big money that took away Gerry Hitchens and myself started the rot. The team changes that followed accelerated it. There were experiments on the wings and at centre-forward Ray Crawford, Ray Pointer and Bobby Smith were all competing. But whatever the cause, I only knew it wasn't the same side that I had left.

Haynes also worried about the effect of Italy on England's star striker:

Jimmy Greaves had been unable to settle in Milan. He was transferred back to Tottenham Hotspur just before Christmas in a welter of publicity that made his original transfer to Italy seem like a ladies' afternoon whist drive. There was little doubt that if he recaptured his form he would be back in the England team [but] I was a little concerned about Jimmy. I saw him three or four times after his return and thought that his general play had improved and I wondered if this was a good thing and whether it might blunt the edge of his goalscoring facility. In

Italy I think he had to play to order, to play deep in midfield or wide on the wings, but he soon recovered his goalscoring touch with the Spurs and I stopped worrying.

Despite these fears ahead of the World Cup, England's draw was to be an encouraging one. Hungary were a strong side, but were nowhere near as gifted as the great team of 1953. Argentina were not a very competent side at that time, and the Bulgarians had qualified by fluke, having got to Chile after upsetting the odds and beating France in the play-off games. Another encouraging thought, of course, was that Greaves had indeed recaptured his goalscoring form on home soil, despite the fact that he and the rest of the England team had only been together for a few weeks before the tournament, whereas teams like Brazil had been training together for two months.

England went to Chile confident that they could at least progress through their group, but they were in for a shock when they lost the first game against the Hungarians on the last day of May by two goals to one. Light rain made the conditions tricky and they played in front of only 10,000 people in a spacious stadium in Rancagua, but nothing could cover up the fact that England had been defeated in a game they never should have lost. It was a terrible start for Winterbottom and his team, but things were about to take a turn for the better in the next match against Argentina on 2 June. The England squad were racked with nerves following their disappointing first outing against Hungary and knew the pressure was on them to achieve a result – which they did, as a proud Johnny Haynes recalled:

The match was to be played on the Queen's birthday, but I doubt if that inspired us. Early in the match, Alan Peacock of Middlesbrough, who had replaced Hitchens at centre-forward, rose perfectly to a Charlton cross. His header had beaten Roma, the Argentine goalkeeper, and was crossing the line when Navarro, their very tough centre-half, handled it clear. Flowers crashed the penalty kick home. Now we had won the first critical goal . . . Bobby Charlton broke inside a few minutes before half-time and hit a typically thoroughbred goal . . . and Jimmy Greaves was on the spot to run in the third.

A goalless draw with the Bulgarians was enough to see England through to the next round against Brazil, the reigning champions, and sure enough the result brought to an end their participation in the competition. Winterbottom's men were beaten 3–1, despite holding the South Americans at 1–1 for a spell during the game. Jimmy Greaves only came close to scoring, hitting the woodwork with a header that ricocheted off the cross-bar and on to the post; Haynes suspected he was trying too hard to win for his country: 'Jimmy Greaves . . . may have been concerned with making sure of his shots instead of flashing a boot at them instinctively as he does with Tottenham, but the plain fact is that he, like the rest of us, did not have adequate preparation.'

Still, it was to be a useful learning curve for the Spurs striker as he continued to develop his skills in the English First Division. Jimmy Greaves had made a name for himself on the international stage as well as on the domestic one, and he was now one of the most feared strikers in world football. His qualities and reputation were to make him a focal player in the plans of Alf Ramsey, who took over from Walter Winterbottom as England manager in 1963, and his experience was vital in England's preparations for the World Cup on home soil.

Sadly, the 1966 World Cup, Greaves' last, was to be tinged with more heartbreak than his experiences with the England team in Chile. And this time the tragedy would be more personal.

12 The World Cup Heartbreak

Of course I was disappointed. Of course I was upset.
Who wouldn't be, for goodness' sake?

JIMMY GREAVES, 1998

Though he has denied it himself, many people pinpoint
Jimmy Greaves' exclusion from the side that contested
the 1966 World Cup final at Wembley as the moment
his interests turned away from football and towards
alcoholism. Greaves himself has indicated the illness
that later ruined his marriage started as a result of his
having to endure a torrid, depressing time in Milan, but
there is no doubt that becoming a peripheral figure at
Spurs in the late 1960s following eight great seasons at
the club and his rejection from the biggest game of his,
or any English player's, life had a damaging effect.

His colleagues suspected so too. 'It haunts me a bit
that it was the start of the slide for Jimmy,' said Geoff
Hurst years later when questioned about the effect on
Greaves of being omitted from the starting line-up of
that historic 1966 team. England midfielder Alan Ball
was equally sympathetic. 'I thought the disappointment
helped to put Jimmy off the rails,' he said. 'Though only
he could say it. He'd set his heart on the World Cup and
Geoff was his deputy.' That Greaves was replaced by
Hurst after three disappointing performances in the
group stages was as much down to bad luck as it was to
an uncharacteristic nervousness in front of goal. In the
first three games against Uruguay, Mexico and France,
Greaves had failed to impress, and when he limped off
after his final game against France with a gash in his
shin, it gave Alf Ramsey the opportunity to employ his

151

understudy in attack. Hurst scored a vital goal against the Argentinians in the quarter-finals, before claiming a historic hat-trick in the final against West Germany. It was a breathtaking performance, but it was an exhibition of skill that could so easily have been performed – if not outclassed – by a match-fit Jimmy Greaves.

For the Spurs striker, the 90 minutes spent on the Wembley sidelines as England claimed their 4–2 victory were to be a case of 'what might have been'. It certainly threw up a mêlée of regrets and speculation as to what could have happened against the Germans had a fully fit Greaves been picked to play over Hurst, a player who, though impressive at club level, had hitherto lacked the big-game experience of international fixtures. Many people thought that Greaves was going to be the natural choice for Ramsey in the final following his absence from the quarter-final and semi-final. The media, especially the London press, were desperate for a Greaves recall, as were the fans, who saw Greaves as more of an entertainer than the powerful and pragmatic Hurst. Even Hurst and his strike partner that day, Roger Hunt, were convinced one of them would be sacrificed in order to accommodate England's star forward. Sadly for Greaves it was not to be. It was a bitter end to a traumatic tournament.

Greaves had experienced problems before a ball had even been kicked in anger at the 1966 World Cup. In December 1965, seven months before the tournament was due to get underway, he was laid low with a nasty bout of hepatitis. Though it wasn't a life-threatening illness (nor one that could be attributed to his fondness for a heavy drinking session), it affected Greaves badly. More worryingly, it had a crippling effect on his game. After making a full recovery, it was apparent that the strengths in his armoury, namely his speed and alertness, were missing. As a result, his first few games back for Spurs in February 1966 were disappointing; Greaves looked a completely different player from the one who had impressed both for England and his club before he was struck down.

These fresh doubts about Greaves' ability to perform at the top level weren't only shared by the player and Spurs manager Bill Nicholson, but by England manager Alf Ramsey. Ramsey had several players in mind for the striker slots in the forthcoming World Cup, including Geoff Hurst, Roger Hunt and John Connelly. Greaves had, of course, been in his plans for the tournament since way back, having enjoyed one of the richest veins of form of his career in the 1964/65 season, scoring 29 times for Spurs in the League and yet again claiming the Division One top scorer title, but Ramsey knew the reserve players in his squad were just as important as the starting eleven in a major tournament and he couldn't afford to take any passengers. Greaves himself, naturally, was worried about his illness, that the toll it might take on his physical strength would be perceived by Ramsey. He was desperate to play in the World Cup in 1966. He knew England would win the tournament, not just because they were competing on home soil in front of a packed Wembley house every game, but because Ramsey had the best England squad for years at his disposal.

Captain Bobby Moore had recovered from injury to reclaim his place in the starting line-up and had earned a reputation as one of the best defenders in the world; with George Cohen of Fulham, Jack Charlton of Leeds and Everton's Ray Wilson, England's defence would be one of the best in the competition. When one considered that none other than Gordon Banks was keeping watch between the sticks, Greaves was convinced England would concede very few goals in the tournament. And while defensively England were strong, they also had teeth in midfield and attack. Nobby Stiles of Manchester United played just in front of the back four and was a tenacious player, allowing the creativity of Alan Ball, Bobby Charlton and Martin Peters to be used to devastating effect, enabling them to feed Liverpool's Roger Hunt up front. The question on Greaves' mind, and on the minds of countless pundits and fans, before the tournament was 'Who would be Roger Hunt's strike partner?'

Fortunately for Greaves, there were few alternative candidates as he battled against illness and performed well enough in the later stages of the 1965/66 season (and during the warm-up trip to Scandinavia, where Greaves hit the back of the net four times in a 6–1 thrashing of Norway) to impress Ramsey and earn his place in the starting line-up for the first game of the 1966 World Cup against Uruguay on 11 July. It was the call-up the public wanted. They saw Jimmy Greaves as a match winner, a player who could turn a game with his anticipation and skill. He was, after all, one of the most exciting players in the world on his day and the World Cup would give him the perfect stage on which to display his talent to the watching world.

The anticipation in the lead-up to the match was incredible, but come the day Wembley was only half full. Despite the Queen's participation in the opening ceremony, thousands of fans opted against travelling to the twin towers, preferring to watch the game on television. Tickets had been sold in bulk, with fans having to buy tickets to all three group games to ensure they could obtain tickets for the quarter-finals. But so confident were the home support of qualification from the group stages that the majority decided to stay in the comfort of their own homes.

The nation expected Uruguay to be dispatched with some ease. Most pundits believed England to be in the easiest group in the tournament, and the Uruguayans were labelled as England's first victims on the road to the quarter-finals, but the South Americans had other ideas and the tournament didn't start as well as Greaves or England would have wanted. Indeed, the home nation's opener was labelled a flop both on and off the pitch. From the opening minutes of the match it was clear the Uruguayans had no intention of taking the game to England, preferring instead to concentrate on stopping the home side from scoring. Physical tackling and a stifling man-marking system shackled the England forwards and strangled the midfield, leaving Greaves very few chances with which to breach the Uruguayan goal. The best opportunity fell to John Connelly, who hit the top of the crossbar with a header. The game ended 0–0, disappointing the home support and angering the national press, who demanded a drastic change in tactics from Ramsey.

Ramsey, however, remained confident about England's chances. He had already predicted England would win the World Cup in the build-up to the competition and knew the Uruguayans would be a difficult side to crack. Greaves, meanwhile, disappointed not to have scored in the opening game, turned his attentions to the next match against Mexico on 16 July. Like the Uruguayans, Mexico seemed determined to stop England from playing rather than taking the game on themselves, but despite having a great deal of experience in international competitions they were unable to choke the English attack. The highlight of the match was Bobby Charlton's goal. Picking up the ball in their own half, the England defenders fed Charlton in the centre of the pitch. Deciding to go on his own, Charlton surged forward, passing a clutch of Mexican defenders on the way before firing the ball home from 25 yards. The game was won, but once again Greaves played a bit part in the match.

The final group match against France was to be an even worse experience for Greaves. Frustrated at not yet getting off the mark in the tournament, he pressed forward at every possible opportunity and as a result was continually caught offside. In addition to his poorly timed runs, Greaves looked uncharacteristically unsure of himself in front of goal, missing a handful of chances he would normally have tucked away in a Spurs shirt. The French, meanwhile, pressed forward and looked a creative and dangerous unit, but Moore's strong leadership in defence was enough to hold them at bay.

If Greaves was unable to get on the scoresheet, he could take heart from the fact that he contributed to England's first goal. Picking up a loose ball on the left wing he fired in a cross which was met by the head of Jack Charlton. It was a powerful header that bounced back off the crossbar and into the path of a grateful Roger Hunt, who passed the ball into an empty net. In the second half England doubled their lead with a move that was again instigated by Jimmy Greaves. Collecting a ball in midfield, Greaves threaded a neat through-ball to Callaghan. The winger fired the ball into the box and Roger Hunt redirected the ball past Aubour, the French goalkeeper, and into the goal. Aubour managed to get his fingertips to the shot, but the ball slipped out of his hands and went over the line.

With this victory England had won their group, and they progressed to the quarter-final stages and what turned out to be a controversial tie against Argentina, but the French game had ended in disaster for Greaves. Going into a tackle, the striker had picked up a nasty gash on his left shin that later required four stitches. The injury would rule him out of the rest of the tournament.

Greaves' bad luck gave Ramsey the opportunity to try out Geoff Hurst in attack alongside Roger Hunt. The West Ham striker had only earned a handful of caps before the tournament, but was considered by Ramsey a suitable replacement for Greaves, who had failed to impress. Hurst, on the other hand, made his mark straight away, scoring the deciding goal in a hard-earned 1–0 victory over an Argentinian side that had little intention of winning the game by fair means. Their captain, Antonio Rattin, had to be physically pulled off the pitch by the police after referee Rudolph Kreitlein of West Germany was forced to send him off. Like England's previous South American opposition in the tournament, Argentina only seemed interested in spoiling the game, slowing down England's tempo with a series of cynical fouls and off-the-ball challenges that incensed the crowd and the England bench. Rattin was the chief culprit; the Argentinian captain, a gifted player in his own right, seemed more interested in influencing the opinion of the referee than having a positive effect on the match with the ball. As a result the game was reduced to a disappointing spectacle marred by the unpleasant tactics of the Argentinians, whom Alf Ramsey would later brand 'animals'.

It was an ugly match, but England's winning goal was a typical Geoff Hurst effort. Looking up into the opposition's half and seeing Martin Peters with the ball at his feet, Hurst instinctively ran towards the near post. Peters could not see his West Ham team-mate's run, but he naturally knew where Hurst would be heading. It was a move they had worked on continually at the Hammers' Chadwell Heath training ground and had used to devastating effect in the First Division. It produced a similar result against Argentina. Curling a ball in from the left wing, Peters' cross was met by a Hurst glancing header after the striker had made a fifteen-yard burst into the box. The ball fizzed past the reach of goalkeeper Roma and into the goal. It was a deadly move that the South Americans had no answer to. They had been bullying Hurst continually in the air with a combination of flying elbows and shirt pulling and were expecting a high ball into the box every time an England player received the ball on the touchline. The short cross to the near post was something they hadn't counted on; nor could they have fully appreciated the depth of understanding between Hurst and Peters. It was enough to win England the game.

From the touchline, Greaves could only watch in despair. He had never been a good spectator, hating it when he was unable to influence a game, and the Argentinians' underhand tactics had made him fidgety to say the least. As the anger swelled in the men on the bench around him he found he could not give the game his full concentration, and when the Argentinian goal was breached at last by Hurst he could only wonder at what effect it would have on his World Cup.

Greaves, of course, was delighted at the fact that Hurst had put England into the semi-finals, but at the same time he was desperate to win his place back. What would the chances of that be now, considering that his replacement had, with one glancing header, scored more goals in one game than he had managed in the tournament's three group games?

Later that week it was obvious to Greaves that while the shin injury was healing it was still causing him problems. He was match fit, but any knock could result in the deep cut bursting open again. In fact, such was the precarious nature of the wound that Greaves could only bathe if his injured shin was propped up out of the water. By the time the semi-final against Portugal came around on 26 July, Greaves was still doubtful, and it looked almost certain that Hurst would get the nod ahead of him again.

The Portuguese came to the match in tremendous form. They'd beaten North Korea 5–3 in the quarter-finals and defeated Hungary, Brazil and Bulgaria in the group stages notching up nine goals in the process, but Ramsey fancied his chances on home soil. He knew the Portuguese would be no pushover, though, and the West Ham striker was his first choice up front. Ramsey wasn't going to risk a three-quarters fit Greaves over a fully fit striker who had worked tirelessly against the Argentinians; it could prove too costly, especially as Hurst was more of a team player than Greaves. The Spurs striker would have to sit on the sidelines again.

Bobby Charlton scored two goals in a dramatic 2–1 win. It was the entertaining game the clash with Argentina should have been had it not been marred by the South Americans' negativity. Greaves sat through another impressive performance from Hurst and Hunt in attack, despite the fact that both goals came from midfield, and was convinced at this stage that he would not be playing in the final; once again he watched from the sidelines as the celebrations erupted around him, knowing that Alf Ramsey would stick with a successful formula.

Others refused to be so sure. In the four days leading up to the final the press launched a campaign to reinstate Greaves to the full line-up. The London print media were particularly vocal in their demands to see Greaves walking out at Wembley on 30 July for the final against West Germany, having followed his career closely at Chelsea and Spurs. The players, meanwhile, carried on as normal, trying to ignore the media circus that was developing around Greaves, Hurst and Hunt – none more so than Geoff Hurst himself.

The papers were full of it. The TV and radio commentators asked the question of themselves and every other sporting personality they could lure into the studios. But nowhere was the question asked more often than at Hendon Hall where England trained, waited and slept.

So I sat and stewed. I had wanted nothing in my life more than I now wanted to play for England in this final. I wanted it so badly I literally ached at the thought of not being in it. And every one of the twenty-two of us locked up in Hendon felt exactly the same as I did. Even those who had not played in the series, and must have known they had no chance of being picked . . . must still have gone on clinging to hope.

It couldn't have been a picnic in Greaves' mind, either. Remember, since he was ten years old Jimmy had never really had to look at a team sheet – he knew his name would always be there. As a youth player, in the League sides of Chelsea and Spurs, it was certain as tomorrow's dawn that when the side was picked it would consist of Greaves and ten others. Years of this must colour a man's thinking . . . now suddenly, probably for the first time in his life, he was wondering, 'Will I be chosen?' And like me I'm sure Jim has never wanted a game in his life so much as he wanted this one.

It was a traumatic time for all three strikers. None of the trio knew which two would be picked to face the Germans, and Ramsey was giving very little away. For the next few days Greaves, Hurst and Hunt sweated it out as the squad went about its business, working as a unit in preparation for the forthcoming final as if nothing out of the ordinary was happening. But every player was living his own personal hell in the run-up to the final selection. That the three forwards were the centre of so much speculation was of little relevance; Ramsey wanted total concentration in the Hendon Hall training camp and wasn't going to let any controversy surrounding the team affect his last-minute plans.

Many people were convinced that Roger Hunt would be a definite starter, even before the tournament. And although he wasn't a crowd favourite (many fans saw him as a clumsy player), Ramsey was an admirer of his tireless running. Despite the heavy praise heaped on him by the manager, Hunt himself wasn't convinced he would be in the starting line-up. In fact, he was convinced he *wouldn't* be picked. 'Quite honestly, none of us thought there would be a change for the final,' said John Connelly after the final. 'But Roger Hunt did think so. He'd personally had a good World Cup, scored goals, worked hard, was popular in the squad. Yet he doubted himself.'

Greaves was not told of Ramsey's decision until the morning of the game, although those that had been picked were told the night before the match, as Hurst recalled:

Alf's not simple. He is too much of a player's man to not know what we were all suffering. But of course he couldn't release the team until he was sure in his mind, and was certain the side he selected would be fit to play. Picking a side then having to change it is bad for morale ... often the public don't realise this ... for a man who gets a game because someone else has gone down with flu can never enter the match in quite the same mood as someone who knows he was first choice.

It was towards the end of training on the Friday that Alf acted, although the news was not announced to the world until noon the next day. I was just wandering towards the touchline when Alf drifted casually over and said: 'Geoff, you will be playing tomorrow. I thought you'd want to know ... but please keep it to yourself. I am not telling the rest.'

Yet despite Ramsey's best-laid plans, Greaves was already aware he was out of the team.

I knew. One day on the coach, I think it was Thursday, I was sitting next to Harold Shepherdson [a member of the backroom staff] on the way back from training, and I said casually, 'I suppose it's going to be difficult to get back [into the team],' and he turned away and looked out of the window. I was close to Harold, he'd been there ever since I came into the squad. Alf had obviously confided in him, and he was too embarrassed to talk to me.

By the time he woke up on the Saturday morning, Greaves knew he was about to hear the awful news. Before breakfast he began to pack his bags, much to the surprise of his room-mate Bobby Moore. Despite the fact he knew he had been picked, Moore was unaware of Greaves' position. Ramsey had told the players to keep their selection secret and had not told the players already on the team sheet of his other selections for the game ahead.

'What are you doing?' enquired Moore.

'Just getting ready for a quick getaway once the match is over,' replied Greaves.

Moore was surprised. 'You can do that tomorrow morning,' he said. 'We'll all be out on the bevvy tonight. Celebrating our World Cup win.'

But Greaves was not going to change his mind. A meeting with Ramsey later on that day confirmed his worst fears. Ramsey explained his reasons for wanting to stick with an unchanged side and hoped Greaves would understand, but the meeting was short and to the point. When it was over, Greaves nodded at his manager.

'They'll win it for you,' he said.

Ramsey remained emotionless. 'I think so,' he eventually said, before walking away to inform the others who had been left out.

Greaves took Ramsey's decision gracefully, but his heart was broken. It was the game he'd dreamt of playing in all his life; now that opportunity had been snatched away from him at the last minute. In the hotel, he tried to sound upbeat, to encourage the players who had been picked, but his enthusiastic words didn't fool anyone. The rest of the squad knew that Greaves was shattered by the announcement, and several of the side later described his face as being as 'long as a Green Line bus'. Greaves later admitted to Kenneth Wolstenholme that of course he'd been distraught at the time: 'To play for your country in the final of the World Cup is the pinnacle of anyone's career, and I missed it. But only eleven Englishmen could make it on the day, and if you want to know whether they did a good job or not, look in the record books.'

The record books, of course, tell us that the day belonged to England, and to Geoff Hurst in particular, but despite his personal disappointment Greaves was not bitter about the affair. As the team celebrated by walking around the pitch following the 4–2 victory, Jack Charlton was seen to put a consoling arm around Greaves' shoulders (a gesture similar to the one Greaves had made to Dave Mackay after Spurs triumphed in the Cup Winners' Cup in 1963 in the Scotsman's absence), but it was of little help. England had won the World Cup in front of their home crowd, and arguably their greatest striker had played little part in it. 'I danced around the pitch with everybody else,' he explained later, 'but even in this great moment of triumph I felt a sickness in my stomach that I had not taken part in the match of a lifetime. It was my saddest day in football.'

That evening, Greaves slipped away quietly as the rest of the squad stayed at the Royal Garden Hotel in London to celebrate. Ramsey was curious as to why Greaves was not present.

'He's not bitter about it,' Moore explained to his manager. 'He just doesn't want to be here. He'd rather be away from it all.'

Greaves himself later admitted to his reasons for not attending: 'I was told later by Mooro that Alf thought I had deliberately snubbed him after the game, but that is far from the truth. I was delighted for Alf and didn't want to spoil his moment of glory by letting him see the hurt in my eyes. I went home and quietly got drunk. Late that night I went on a family holiday. The 1966 World Cup was suddenly history.'

Greaves had given some of the best years of his career to England. This rejection before the hugest of games had broken his heart.

13 A Last Taste of Glory

*Gilly and Greavsie were working so well together at that
point. By the start of the 1966/67 season they were one of
the most feared partnerships in the country. They were
nicknamed the G-Men, and they were the goalscorers
and the golden boys of the team.*

ALAN MULLERY, 2000

With the break-up of the Spurs team in 1964 and the
consequent need to rebuild, the north London club had
found itself in a long period of transition. For the White
Hart Lane faithful, who had been spoilt with success in
the early years of the decade in both domestic and
European competition, Nicholson's reconstruction programme was a frustrating period. Gone were crowd
favourites, players of the calibre of Danny Blanchflower, John White and Bobby Smith. Cliff Jones was
also reaching the end of his career, and the new players
such as Pat Jennings and Alan Mullery were finding it
difficult to live up to the expectations of a crowd used
to glory.

Their League performances weren't bad by anyone
else's standards, it was just that they weren't good
enough for a Tottenham used to trophies. Spurs finished fourth in 1964, sixth in 1965 and eighth in 1966, and
while these League placements would have been good
enough for most fans, they left the White Hart Lane
regulars dreaming impatiently of the good old days.
Mullery recalled:

> Bill was building for the future and he could see the
> Double-winning side breaking up in 1964, so he

bought all these young players like myself, Pat Jennings and Cyril Knowles. Other players like Joe Kinnear had been brought through the youth ranks and we were all babies really. We certainly weren't experienced enough to deal with all the expectation at first. In 1961 we'd won the League and FA Cup and in 1962 the FA Cup again and the Cup Winners' Cup in 1963, so to not win anything for four years was understandably frustrating for the fans.

But for a transitional period we did OK. We played really well and didn't finish outside the top five that often and we were fairly consistent. There was a lot of pressure on us at that point to match the achievements of before, especially for Greavsie because he had to score the goals, but he took it in his stride. It never put him off his game and he scored goals for fun.

In fact, Greaves was having such a good time that he'd managed to finish top goalscorer in the First Division in 1963/64 (with 35 goals) and 1964/65 (with 29 goals), despite the fact that Spurs failed to pick up a trophy in that time; his tally for the season after that, 1965/66, was only lower because he'd contracted hepatitis and was out of the game for several months. 'He was a wonderful player at that time,' said Mullery.

And although we weren't winning trophies, Jimmy managed to entertain and we were an entertaining team. He was the most consistent goalscorer I've ever seen. In fact, he was so good, he could tell you when he was going to score. I remember we were playing during the end of the 1966/67 season and we needed to beat Stoke to finish third. In those days the club had promised us a £300 bonus to finish in the top three. Greavsie hadn't had a kick all game. Not a kick. There was only fifteen minutes to go and I ran up to him and said, 'Greavsie, £300 might not mean a lot to you, but it means a hell of a lot to me. How about getting us a goal?' And he looked at me and said, 'Well, if you get the ball up to me, I'll win it for you.' I think he got one touch five minutes later and the ball was in the back of the net. We won the match one–nil and we all got our bonus.

I don't think Jimmy carried that side through the transitional period. He was a tremendous player, but there were a lot of tremendous players in the side, it's just that we were finding our feet at the time and we were still a pretty good team despite the fact we didn't win a trophy for a few years. But he was a very important part of that team. We still had players like Dave Mackay who had recovered from two broken legs, and he was one of the best players I've ever seen, and it was obvious that Bill was building a side to match the Double team of 1961. A lot of us found it difficult at first, especially me. I'd been brought in to replace Danny Blanchflower in 1964, which is something of a task in itself, but once Dave Mackay broke his leg for the second time shortly afterwards, I had to replace both of them! How do you do that? They were two world-class players and of course nobody could replace them, but after six or seven months I won the fans over and settled in like the rest of us.

We finished third in the 1966/67 season, but we had a tremendous Cup run. Before that point we never really dropped out of the top six, but we hadn't won anything for four years and that simply was not good enough. Not for Tottenham anyway. 1966/67 was the season we had to win something to ease the pressure. People were getting on our backs and we had to do something about it. I remember the team meeting at the start of that season at Cheshunt [Spurs' training ground at the time] and Bill Nicholson said something along the lines of, 'It doesn't matter how we play this year, as long as we win something. If we win a trophy we're OK because it means next season we can get back into Europe.' And it was important that we were competing in Europe because we had set the standard in 1963 and had to live up to it.

The season was an important one personally for Jimmy Greaves as well. All eyes were on him following the heartbreak of non-selection for the 1966 World Cup final, and it was important for both the player and his club that he bounced back quickly. In some quarters there were those still concerned that the bout of hepatitis he'd suffered the season before might have affected him in the long term, and they kept a keen eye on him, searching for any deficiencies in his game. Well, he bagged 25 goals that season – not a bad haul by anyone's standards – helping his club to third place in the League, and in the FA Cup he made his mark again, as the partnership with Alan Gilzean began to flourish.

The early excitement Greaves had felt at being partnered with 'Gilly' had now spread to the rest of the squad, as the G-Men (as they were nicknamed by fans and the national press) became one of the most feared forward duos in the League. It was a combination that was to reap dividends for Nicholson that year, as Alan Mullery confirmed:

Gilly and Greavesie worked together so well. They had always looked strong together, but in 1967 they helped us to win something, which was important for the club because we had lost the Bobby Smith and Jimmy Greaves combination and needed someone to spark off the team. Bill bought Gilly and they hit it off straight away. It was a wonderful partnership and it really flowed that season. Gilly was a wonderful player and together they were brilliant . . . They got all the headlines. When you're playing well as a team, you're always going to need a strong partnership up front to finish things off, and they gave us that.

Spurs' FA Cup run started on 28 January at the old Den, and while it wasn't the most glamorous of starts, it proved to be a tough opening tie. Millwall were a useful team at the time, plying their trade in the Second Division, having been promoted from the Third the previous season. Like most newly promoted clubs they were enjoying themselves in the higher divisions, cutting their teeth on more superior opposition and claiming the odd scalp along the way. But Millwall weren't merely along for the ride. They eventually finished eighth that season and were looking to take Spurs down in the FA Cup.

The Spurs players (and fans) were more concerned about the venue than the opposition. The Den and its supporters had a reputation as one of the most intimidating cauldrons in the League, and the crowd factor played an important role in the game, as Alan Mullery remembered:

> We played in front of 42,000 at Millwall on the Saturday at the Den and they had to shut the gates about an hour before kick-off because so many people had turned up to watch the game. We got a 0–0 result, which we were pleased with because Millwall is never an easy place to get a result. The fans are so intimidating and Millwall were a useful side in those days. We took them back to White Hart Lane the following Wednesday and another 60,000 turned up to watch us win 1–0, with Gilly getting us the goal. I think that first game against Millwall was the toughest we had in the competition. If you've ever been there you'll know it used to be a nightmare place to go and get a result.

If Spurs found this third-round tie a mentally demanding game, the next two matches were to be a stroll in the park. Portsmouth were demolished 3–1 at White Hart Lane on 18 February. Then Greaves' side lucked out with another home draw against lower League opposition when Bristol City were pulled out of the hat. The struggling Second Division club were swept aside 2–0, leaving Spurs to face what turned out to be a controversial sixth-round tie against Birmingham City at St Andrews on 8 April. City were a mid-table Second Division club and should have been an easy conquest for the First Division giants, but they had other ideas and Spurs found themselves hanging on for a 0–0 draw. Still, despite the scoreline, the match was filled with excitement as Spurs nearly found themselves out of the competition when goalkeeper Pat Jennings dropped a Birmingham cross on his goal line. The City players were adamant the ball had crossed the line, but the referee, not having a clear view of the incident, waved play on.

It was the stroke of luck Tottenham needed. The replay at White Hart Lane on 12 April turned into a massacre. Spurs, determined not to experience a repeat performance of the first game, came out hungry for victory. Two early goals from Terry Venables quashed any hopes the Second Division side may have had of an upset, before goals from Frank Saul, Alan Gilzean and a brace from Jimmy Greaves completed a 6–0 win.

Greaves, while pleased with the Spurs performance, immediately turned his attention to the semi-final draw and was concerned at the quality of the opposition still in the bag. Whoever Spurs drew would be tricky opposition; there were no easy ties left. Leeds United, arguably one of the strongest sides in the country and about to embark on a decade of powerful and successful football, sat alongside Tommy Docherty's useful Chelsea side and an in-form Nottingham Forest, who were to finish second in the League behind Manchester United that year. There was no easy route to Wembley there.

Forest were twinned with Spurs, and it proved to be an interesting fixture. Chasing United for the League title at the time, Forest were in with a genuine chance of emulating Tottenham's ground-breaking Double of 1961. Jimmy Greaves was looking forward to the match. For some reason he always seemed to play well against Nottingham Forest; he'd scored 24 goals against them throughout his career to date – in fact, they were the side he scored the most goals against as a professional footballer. Given Greaves' confidence, Spurs fancied their chances, and the odds were tipped in their favour when Forest's key player, Joe Baker, revealed that he couldn't play following a knock sustained in their quarter-final tie against Everton. Things were looking rosy for Greaves and Spurs.

Knowing his penchant for hitting the back of their net, Forest would have been forgiven for keeping Greaves on a tight leash, shackling him for the full 90 minutes in an attempt to prevent him from scoring. They didn't, and on the half-hour mark the G-Men struck to devastating effect. Forest had been dominating the game to that point, but then a long clearance from Spurs centre-half Mike England was flicked on by Alan Gilzean. It was a move that had been used regularly in the League, and now Gilly's unerring ability to glance a header into the path of Greaves was to work yet again. The ball dropped down by his left boot and, twisting sharply, Greaves struck the ball on the half volley. It was a grass-cutter and not the most well-executed of shots from someone renowned for his ability in front of goal, but the ball skimmed over the turf for 25 yards before ricocheting in off the post. Frank Saul scored a second late on in the second half. Forest grabbed their first with minutes remaining, but it was too late. Tottenham were in their third FA Cup final of the decade.

Their opponents on 20 May were to be Chelsea, who, under Tommy Docherty's canny stewardship, had earned themselves a reputation as a talented team of promising youngsters. Spurs had already lost to Chelsea 3–0 at Stamford Bridge that season (their heaviest defeat that year) and had only been able to manage a draw with the west Londoners in the return fixture at White Hart Lane. Bill Nicholson was concerned before the game that his side would struggle against their London rivals, but it wasn't just the players who had the game on their mind. It was the first all-London final in the FA Cup's long and proud history, and the clash between Chelsea and Spurs quickly became the talk of pubs and cafés around the capital, as Joe Kinnear, who had broken into the Spurs team at the start of the campaign, recalled:

> There was a brilliant atmosphere during the weeks leading up to it. Not just at White Hart Lane, but everywhere you went in London, people were talking about it. The week before we all went to a dinner at the Hilton Hotel, an Anglo-American Sporting Club event. It was a boxing club, which put on big posh dinners. They'd invited both the Cup Final teams so we found ourselves sitting at the same table, opposite the Chelsea lads. I don't think they'd meet like that today. Terry Venables, who had joined us the May before, had of course played for Chelsea. He knew most of their players, so we were all soon chatting and joking. The Cup itself was there, on show at the dinner. I remember looking at it and wondering if it would be ours or Chelsea's.

With both clubs hailing from the capital, the match developed into a psychological drama with each manager applying his own form of kidology. Docherty, as you might expect, was keen to talk his side up, while Nicholson preferred to keep quiet about the game and let his players do the talking on the pitch. Even the players became involved in the mental game of cat and mouse, but according to Greaves, before the game was played it was apparent who had come out on top.

> There was something odd about that match. It was as if we knew before a ball was kicked that we were the

winners. It showed most of all in the tunnel at Wembley just before the two teams walked out on the pitch. Chelsea 'looked' a beaten side. They were frozen like statues, while we were relaxed and talking amongst ourselves. What had made us so confident was that we had gone 28 matches without defeat, a run that had started on New Year's Eve [1966]. We finished third in the League and would have pulled off the Double again had we started our winning ways just a couple of games earlier.

Alan Mullery also remembered the atmosphere in that Wembley tunnel:

Although Chelsea had beaten us at Stamford Bridge and we only managed a draw at White Hart Lane, they looked petrified. In fact, Dave Mackay turned round to us and said, 'Look at this lot. We've beaten them already. They don't fancy it.' And he was right. They did look beaten. They were only young kids at the time and we looked at them and we knew we were winners. We knew they were a useful side and a young side, but we had experience on the big stage and they didn't. Greavsie had been there with England and it was Dave Mackay's third final, so we had loads of experience, and in the end it showed.

By this stage, Bill Nicholson had also come round to the same view, that his side had a definite psychological edge over their opponents – and when he read about the Chelsea line-up in the hours before kick-off he realised they had the tactical edge too.

I believe Tommy Docherty made a tactical mistake before the 1967 FA Cup final which made our task easier in the first all-London final. Docherty was then in his heyday, cracking jokes and constantly appearing in the newspapers as he guided his young side towards Wembley. In previous matches he used Martin Hinton as a sweeper and took three out of four points in League matches. Alan Gilzean did not like playing against a sweeper, and it showed in these matches.

But just before the final, Docherty abandoned the idea and played an orthodox defensive system. When I heard that, I told my players: 'He's done us a favour.' Docherty was a good coach but he was impulsive and changed his mind a lot.

Nicholson's judgement was to be proved right. Docherty had indeed done Spurs a favour by not playing the sweeper system, but the opening 45 minutes of the final weren't as comfortable as the Spurs team might have imagined in the players' tunnel. Chelsea may have been a young side, but they were also strong and a good match for the Spurs line-up, with Peter 'The Cat' Bonetti in goal, Alan Harris, Eddie McCreadie, John Hollins, Marvin Hinton, Ron Harris, Charlie Cooke, Tommy Baldwin, Tony Hateley, Bobby Tambling and John Boyle. But the Spurs team – Pat Jennings, Joe Kinnear, Cyril Knowles, Alan Mullery, Mike England, Dave Mackay, Jimmy Robertson, Alan Gilzean, Terry Venables and Frank Saul, with Greavsie completing Nicholson's starting eleven – certainly had more big-game experience. (There was even more experience on the Spurs bench. This year's FA Cup final was the first to allow a substitute; the role for Tottenham was filled that day by Cliff Jones.)

The game started off on an even keel, both teams attacking in equal measure. Luck was definitely against Chelsea when in the sixth minute Eddie McCreadie tore ligaments in his shoulder while stretching for a header. Bonetti was looking strong in goal, however, and worryingly for Spurs, Ron 'Chopper' Harris was making a good job of neutralising Greaves in attack. The striker was shadowed the entire game, but he still looked dangerous. Chelsea had very obviously pinpointed Greaves as Spurs' greatest threat, and were attempting to snuff it out completely.

Just before half-time Spurs got the break they needed. Following a Chelsea attack which nearly resulted in a goal, Mullery picked up the ball in defence. Pushing forward, the midfielder surged on into the Chelsea half before striking a shot goalwards. The ball cannoned off Greavsie's shadow for the afternoon, Harris, and into the path of Jimmy Robertson, who swept the ball beyond Bonetti. Spurs were one up, and from that moment on they shut Chelsea out of the game. Twenty minutes into the second half and they were two up following an incredible stroke of good fortune. Picking up a loose ball on the edge of the Chelsea area, Frank Saul lashed it towards the goal. It soared past Bonetti and into the top corner. The Cat didn't even see it coming. Saul would later admit that he'd had no idea where the ball was heading until he saw it in the back of the net. A Bobby Tambling goal with four minutes remaining came too late for Chelsea, and once again Spurs and Jimmy Greaves were parading the FA Cup around Wembley.

COCKERELS COAST THROUGH COCKNEY FINAL proclaimed the *Telegraph*.

In the first all-London FA Cup final this century, Spurs enjoyed a much easier victory over Chelsea than the 2–1 scoreline suggests. It was their third cup win in the sixties, but only two men remained from their previous success in 1962 – Dave Mackay and Jimmy Greaves. Bill Nicholson has built another fine footballing side after the break-up of the 'double' team, the heart of which was wrenched out with the retirement of Blanchflower, the death of John White and the serious injuries to Mackay. But Mackay's undoubted courage has never been better demonstrated than by his double comeback, and it was entirely appropriate that he should lead the new Spurs to their latest triumph.

Spurs seemed to stroll through the match, always in control, individually and collectively superior to a Chelsea side they never allowed into the game. Up front, Greaves and Gilzean were always dangerous; at the back England was dominant. Chelsea's few threats came from Charlie Cooke's exciting but erratic dribbling.

Tommy Docherty would later claim that Spurs had been lucky, while Bill Nicholson again rollicked his players for not being entertaining enough, as Venables remembered: 'Bill Nicholson gave a serious speech about winning the Cup Final, saying that we had not played that well, putting us down, which was not necessarily what we wanted to hear at that particular moment and Dave [Mackay] shouted out, 'Sit down, Bill, you're pissed!' It was typical of Bill, that he was unable to relax and unwind, even on the night of the Cup Final, but was already thinking and worrying about the season ahead.'

But for the players and Jimmy Greaves the pressure had been taken off Spurs with that FA Cup win. The fans were happy with another trophy and the critics had been silenced. There would be no more mention of the Super Spurs side of 1961. 'It certainly took the pressure off us a little bit,' said Alan Mullery. 'There was always going to be a huge expectation for us to win things because of what had happened before, and we'd finally done it after four years. But it didn't relax Bill Nicholson. He was never relaxed because he wanted to repeat the achievements of before. He set high standards for himself.'

Though he didn't know it at the time, it was also a watershed moment in Jimmy Greaves' career. Bill Nicholson constantly thought ahead, forever striving to win more trophies with Spurs, and he was looking to improve the side he had. The Yorkshireman was already intending to begin looking to pastures new for a fresh young striker. Though it pained him, he knew his star striker might have only one or two good seasons left in him at the top level, and he had to think of the club's future.

Greavsie had not only just won his last piece of silverware with Tottenham Hotspur, he'd just won the last of his career.

14 Greavsie Goes Bananas

I found my concentration drifting more and more towards my business affairs, and it was in the back of my mind to jack the game in at the end of the season.

JIMMY GREAVES, 1972

Once again, Spurs' domestic success meant they were eligible for the 1967/68 European Cup Winners' Cup competition, and Bill Nicholson was desperate to repeat the success of 1963. His Tottenham side had shaken off the press criticism following their win in the FA Cup at Wembley and Nicholson was keen to ensure they remained enthusiastic about their fortunes at home and abroad. Sadly, for Nicholson and Greaves, Spurs were knocked out in the early stages of the tournament by Olympique Lyonnaise of France.

'Our first-round opponents were the Yugoslav team Hadjuk Split, which is based in a seaside town the size of Walsall not far from Dubrovnik,' Nicholson wrote later.

It was a relaxing trip with good weather, and although we won 2–0, Hadjuk were a very strong side. The highlight was the way in which the crowd in the primitive ground threw fireworks and crackers on to the pitch, frequently forcing the referee to halt play. At the end they set fire to the trainer's bench, but we had left our seats by then! We were rather slack in the second leg and allowed the Yugoslavs to pull back to 4–3 after being 3–0 down.

The second round paired us with the French club Olympique Lyonnaise whom we should have beaten because they were rated as one of the poorer sides in France. The Municipal de Gerland Stadium had a capacity of 45,000 but there were only 10,000 fans present at the start. They made up for their lack of numbers with boisterous support which soon spilled over into violence and invasions of the pitch.

Spurs lost that first leg 1–0, and although they were confident of reversing the tie at White Hart Lane, they only beat the Frenchmen 4–3 and went out on the away goals rule.

The domestic season had got off to a bad start too. It was a League campaign that Jimmy Greaves would later describe as the unhappiest of his career. He was concerned by his form and felt he was not getting the best out of his game. Maybe he was jaded from the combination of the World Cup in 1966 followed by a long season without a suitable break in which to recharge himself. Maybe he was still feeling the effects of the hepatitis that had struck him down two years previously. Whatever the reason, he wasn't the player that had strutted around the penalty areas of White Hart Lane for the past five seasons with the confidence of someone who knew he could score goals for fun. Greaves was tired, but more worrying than the fatigue was his sudden lack of interest in the game. 'It was during that season that I first considered early retirement from the game,' he confessed later. 'I found the snap had gone right out of my game. I wasn't enjoying my football and suffered bouts of depression because of it.'

Bill Nicholson had also noticed the lack of spark in his striker and went shopping in an attempt to rejuvenate Greaves. Martin Chivers was bought for a then club record of £125,000, but the striker found it difficult to settle in a Spurs shirt and could not form the sort of partnership the team had been used to when Greavsie was with Bobby Smith or Alan Gilzean. Nicholson also decided, braving the wrath of the Spurs crowd, to sell Dave Mackay to Derby and Cliff Jones to Fulham.

Greaves found it increasingly difficult to adjust to these changes and notched up one of the lowest goal tallies of his career, scoring 23 times throughout the 1967/68 campaign. It was clear something had to be done.

During the close season, Greaves knew he had to make good use of the time and make a decision about his career. Retirement was on his mind, but he felt that if he could just find that spark again, that edge in his game that had made him such a revelation over the last decade, there were still a few good seasons left in him. But a sacrifice would have to be made. Signing an extension to his current Tottenham contract, Greaves decided to opt out of England training squads in order to concentrate on his club career. 'I was in two minds whether to retire or have another season or two,' Greaves mused. 'There was also the thought that a move might be of benefit both to Tottenham and myself. Anyway, I decided to sign a new contract with Tottenham and have another crack at seeing if I could recapture the old form.'

He'd only appeared for his country on three occasions since the World Cup, scoring just the once in the process, but still the news caused a flurry of controversy. The announcement would later come back to haunt him, but to the Spurs striker at the time it made sense. He was still regularly being named in the national squad, but he was offering England little more than an extra body in the training camp. Greaves explained to Ramsey that while it was an honour and a pleasure to play for England, he would rather not join the training sessions unless he was going to be selected for the starting eleven. He wanted to concentrate on rejuvenating himself physically, reserving energy for his club commitments. It seemed like a logical solution for Greaves and certainly wasn't a snub to Ramsey or England, although the national coach would later take it that way.

The combination of a renewed contract and a break from international duty certainly did the trick: in the

1968/69 season Greaves weighed in with 27 League goals, 36 in all competitions, as Spurs finished sixth in the table. It was the change in attitude that had helped Greaves more than any other significant factor in his game. A burden had been taken from his shoulders after his announcement to Ramsey, and although he still loved the club, his performances for Tottenham didn't weigh on his mind as much as they had done in the past. In short, Greavsie had managed to shake off the depression that had afflicted him whenever he was unable to hit the target, and this new relaxed attitude enabled him to play to the best of his ability. Football had become a joy once again, and the goals were coming as quickly and as easily as they had done at any time in his career.

This Indian summer had a negative effect, however. As the Greavsie goals came thick and fast, the press bandwagon for the resumption of his international career gathered momentum.

There was quite a campaign in the press for my reinstatement. Alf – now Sir Alf – was moved to say: 'I am being crucified because I am not selecting Greaves, yet he had told me he does not want to play for England.' I was astonished by that statement because deep down I still wanted to play for my country and, despite what some people might have thought, was always passionately proud to wear the white shirt of England ... Alf completely misunderstood me if he really did believe that I had asked him not to select me to play for England any more. What I had said to Alf during my last training session at Roehampton was that I would rather not be called up unless I was going to play.

At the time, Alf had got into the habit of including me in his training squad and then not naming me to play in the match. He told me it was useful to have a player of my experience on the sidelines. All it did was frustrate me, and as quite an active businessman in those days, I knew there were plenty of things I could have been doing rather than continually waste hours at training get-togethers which for me had no end product.

Greaves remained in the international wilderness, but at least it allowed him to concentrate on another season at White Hart Lane. Sadly for the 29-year-old, it was to be his last in the famous lilywhite shirt of Tottenham Hotspur. Bill Nicholson's side were struggling in the League (Spurs' final position for the 1969/70 campaign would be a disappointing eleventh), Greaves was unable to match the form of the previous year and the mediocre performances were beginning seriously to concern the Spurs manager.

The lowlight of the season came in an FA Cup tie on 28 January 1970. Crystal Palace, newly promoted to the First Division but struggling in the top flight, had been drawn against Spurs. Palace were expected to roll over for a Spurs side with a great deal of experience in the FA Cup, but the south Londoners had other ideas and shocked Spurs with a 1–0 win at Selhurst Park. The press went to town on Nicholson's players, criticising their performance and urging the manager to clear out the dead wood in his side. Cyril Knowles, Alan Gilzean and Joe Kinnear were dropped for the next match, as was Greaves. Knowles, Gilzean and Kinnear all made swift returns to the starting line-up, but Greaves was left on the sidelines for the remainder of the season. That dreadful Palace game was his last for Spurs.

'I cannot say when I first noticed a decline in Jimmy Greaves,' Bill Nicholson wrote later.

In his later years with Tottenham he had built up quite a successful business with his brother-in-law and devoted more time to it . . . Greaves had more bad luck (as well as his omission from the World Cup-winning team) when he contracted hepatitis, which is a very debilitating illness for an athlete. Research into sportsmen's injuries and illness is very limited in Britain and we know very little about the subject. With Greaves, the after-effects of hepatitis must have hastened his decline ... By this time his reactions had slowed. Reflexes are the first thing to go in a footballer, and he relied heavily on them.

As Greaves' absence from the Spurs side stretched from weeks to months, he became something of an albatross around Bill Nicholson's neck. The press questioned the club about his omission from the starting line-up week in, week out. Greaves was determined to steer clear of any controversy and decided to keep his mouth shut every time a journalist put something to him on the subject. But as the weeks passed and the season drew to a close, he became frustrated at his long-drawn-out stint in the reserves and asked his manager about the prospects for his future. Greaves suggested it was probably the right time for him to make a move. Though he undoubtedly felt the same way, Nicholson was loath to sell a player who had given him such loyal service, but he knew it was the only thing for him to do. Greaves certainly wouldn't settle for a career in the reserves with the occasional game in the first team, and all the while he was sat on the sidelines Nicholson was being hounded by the press. Not for the first time in his career, the Spurs manager was in a no-win situation.

While Nicholson was considering his player's future, Greaves decided to turn his attention to an alternative career: rally driving. A race had been organised by the *Daily Mirror* that summer, the destination Mexico. Greaves knew he would not be considered for inclusion in the 1970 World Cup squad so he decided to get there via an alternative route and an alternative sport. Nicholson, aware of his player's love for life behind the wheel of a rally car and needing a bit of extra time to concentrate on sorting out the striker's future as the transfer gossip raged around him, allowed Greaves to play for Tottenham on a part-time basis so as to give him the time to practise for the forthcoming race.

'I used to train just on Tuesdays and Thursday evenings and spend the day either driving or at my business,' Greaves recalled. 'It was probably my first big step towards retirement. Football was pushed down my list of priorities and I began to think more and more about making a complete break from the game. But I considered what Dave Mackay had done for himself with a change of club and wondered if a change would restore my appetite.' And the offers for his services were coming in thick and fast.

Joe Mercer of Manchester City was the first to approach Spurs, and he was followed by Brian Clough of Derby. Clough was offering Greaves the chance to reunite with his old team-mate Dave Mackay, but when that offer came in the striker felt the next season was too far off to make a serious commitment, and anyway, Ford had already offered him a spot on their team for the World Cup Rally. Clough lost interest, as did Nicholson, who saw Greaves' obsession with the motor car as a sign that his interest in and passion for football was slowly disappearing.

Then Martin Peters suddenly became available at West Ham. The World Cup-winning midfielder appealed to the Spurs manager who thought Peters would fit nicely into his plans for the forthcoming season. West Ham manager Ron Greenwood set a price of £200,000 for the player and Nicholson promptly handed over £146,000, the remaining £54,000 to be accounted for by a player swap. Jimmy Greaves was now a West Ham employee.

The move appealed to Greaves. He had friends at West Ham and the club was situated quite near to his house, so he wouldn't have to worry about moving or leaving his business interests behind, as he would have had to do had he joined Clough and Mackay at Derby. West Ham were also playing an attractive form of football at the time, and he was told that if he signed straight away he could concentrate all his efforts on the rally. Following a brief meeting with Ron Greenwood at White Hart Lane on 16 March 1970 during the negotiations for Peters, Greaves made his pledge to Upton Park.

'I don't think the rally was an indication his love of the game was waning,' said Alan Mullery, recalling Greaves' move to Upton Park.

Jimmy always had a lot of interests outside the game, but he still loved football. He was one of the first players to set up business interests in his spare time; he was very shrewd. Of course, we were all shocked when Bill decided to sell him and we thought it was a bad move at first. He was still a great player after all. The press and the fans got at him a little bit, especially when we weren't doing well or struggling to score goals, but we got over it in the end.

'If anybody asked me what was the toughest thing I have had to do in life – apart from trying to give up the drink – I would have to say without hesitation, "Driving in the 1970 World Cup Rally",' said Greaves, recalling his time spent behind a steering wheel in 1970. It was not only tough, but dangerous. If his sale by Tottenham Hotspur had effectively ended his career in top-flight football, the World Cup Rally nearly put an end to his life. The football world was amazed that a player of Greaves' calibre should compete in such a demanding event, and many expected him to fail miserably, but he was to defy the odds and prove himself a hardened competitor.

Ninety-six cars began the race, which set off from Wembley Stadium, and the course took in two continents and 25 countries. Sir Alf Ramsey started the race, which had attracted a huge amount of publicity owing to the high-profile nature of one of the drivers. Greaves was partnered with Tony Fall, an experienced professional who had enjoyed a huge amount of success in the sport. Fall was to be the lead driver, with Greaves his back-up and guide. It was a huge relief for everyone concerned that Fall had experience in abundance, for the World Cup Rally was a gruelling one. This time round it claimed the lives of one driver, a rally official and a young cyclist along the way, and out of the 96 starters only 23 finished the race. Greaves and Fall were among them, finishing in an impressive sixth place.

Despite their high ranking, the 16,245-mile journey wasn't without its problems. Earthquakes in Serbia, tropical floods, landslides and precarious mountain drives were among the 'hitches' experienced by the duo. At times Greaves wondered what on earth he had let himself in for.

How I survived in one piece I will never know. Thanks mainly to the brilliance of my co-driver, Tony Fall, we finished sixth in our black and white Ford Escort that I thought several times would become our hearse.

We used to go 55 hours in one stretch without sleep as we navigated the toughest terrain in the world, driving at speeds of up to 100 mph on mountain roads that were built with only donkey transport in mind. I conscientiously followed the rule of the road, 'Don't Drink and Drive', and the only alcohol I consumed during the rally was while we were on the flight across to Rio after we had tackled the mountains of Serbia in the European half of the event.

Mind you, there were plenty of terrifying times when I wanted to turn to the bottle for comfort.

Greaves and Fall completed the race the day after England skipper Bobby Moore had been flown back to the England camp in Mexico City from Bogotá after being wrongfully arrested for the theft of a bracelet. Greaves was keen to gatecrash the England camp to wish his friends luck and soon found his way into their high-security hotel. He shimmied over a wall to avoid the attentions of the guards who were patrolling the grounds, but was nevertheless quickly accosted as he made his way through the hotel gardens. He had been granted permission to visit the England camp, but wanted to give his new team-mate Moore a surprise by turning up unannounced. After explaining who he was, Greaves was allowed access to the hotel, and he went straight up to see Moore, who was having a quiet night in.

'Where's that bracelet, Mooro?' Greaves shouted as his friend opened the door in surprise.

It had been a difficult time for the England captain, but the arrival of his new team-mate cheered him immensely. Greaves and Moore had always been good friends. It was a friendship that was about to become even stronger at Upton Park.

Sadly, it was also a time when both would realise they were fast approaching the twilight of their careers.

15 The End of an Era

*I was receiving nothing mind-boggling from West Ham,
but the thought of joining Mooro and Geoff Hurst and the
fact that the Hammers' training ground was just a
fifteen-minute drive from my home and businesses lulled
me into a signing I have regretted ever since.*

JIMMY GREAVES, 1979

In the spring of 1970, West Ham United were in a
slump. Ron Greenwood and his side were in the midst
of a relegation battle when Jimmy Greaves arrived
from White Hart Lane in March. The striker was
expected to pull the east London club out of the
quagmire.

How the team could find themselves in such a
predicament puzzled those behind the scenes at the
club. After all, they had three World Cup winners in the
squad in the shape of Martin Peters, Geoff Hurst and
Bobby Moore. Surely they should be challenging for
honours with a trio of players like that? To outsiders,
however, the problem was far clearer: West Ham may
have had some pretty impressive players in their
line-up, but the experienced footballers in the side such
as Moore were coming towards the end of their careers
and were feeling the pace. The remainder of the team
was made up of home-grown youngsters such as Trevor
Brooking or players of the calibre of Hurst and Peters
who found the team-mates around them lacking in
ability and their own games suffering as a result.

Strangely, things had seemed so different in the
summer of 1969, and the season had started well for
Greenwood's men, with two wins in the first two

games. Talk had turned to a good League campaign for the Hammers and the possibility of silverware. The brisk start, though, had soon taken a nosedive as their form dwindled. Clyde Best, a striker who had been brought in from Bermuda, made his debut at the start of the season, but it took him a month to get off the mark, and despite his opening strike in the 4–2 League Cup win against Halifax it was apparent he was struggling in front of goal. West Ham's Cup hopes were then shattered by Nottingham Forest in the next round, and not long after that they were dumped out of the FA Cup by Middlesbrough at Ayresome Park. The goals dried up and Greenwood's team was languishing in seventeenth place by Christmas.

With an injury to Trevor Brooking putting a major dent in the team's plans, it was clear something drastic had to be done, and quickly, as many pundits continued to wonder out loud how a team with three world-class players could play so badly. The fans were also left scratching their heads, and they scratched them again in March when the club delivered a bombshell: Martin Peters, one of the crowd favourites, was on his way to White Hart Lane. It was a deal that would upset a majority of the Upton Park faithful, but their anger was soon soothed by the announcement of the arrival of Jimmy Greaves in exchange for their prized midfielder. Greaves was still regarded by many as one of the best goalscorers in the country, despite the fact he was obviously past his peak. It was felt, inside and outside the game, that a move could spark off a Greavsie revival, just as the renewed contract at White Hart Lane and his 'retirement' from England training had done in 1968. People felt he was the man to ease the club's apparent nerves in front of goal and save West Ham from going down.

For Greaves, it was a move of convenience. He had several friends at the club, most notably Bobby Moore and Geoff Hurst, and knew he would be able to fit into the team quite easily. What's more, the move wouldn't unsettle him in any way as he lived a stone's throw away from the club's facilities. The striker thought he was making an excellent move, but 'Now that I look back and see everything in focus without studying life through the bottom of a glass, I can clearly discern where and when I made my biggest mistakes . . . I agreed to leave Tottenham; I cocked a deaf ear to approaches from Brian Clough; I agreed to join West Ham.'

Greaves later confessed that he had not been thinking straight when he agreed to join Moore, Hurst and co. His attentions at the time were clearly focused on preparations for the World Cup Rally and he saw West Ham as an easy way to see out his career. And it wasn't money that had swayed him either: 'I knew I could have done a lot better financially because I'd had several very tasty offers made on the old hush-hush while I was out of the Tottenham team. Those people who seem to think I made a fortune out of football may be interested and perhaps surprised to learn that never throughout my career did I earn a basic wage of more than £100 a week.' It just seemed the perfect move at the time, but things quickly turned sour.

For the first time in his career, Greaves found himself struggling as he battled to come to terms with the hardships of a relegation dogfight. He immediately began to regret the shift across London, even though his appearance at the club did spark off the hoped-for revival. Bang to form, Greaves scored on his debut during a 5–1 thrashing of Manchester City at Maine Road. He was on the scoresheet after just ten minutes, then added a second fifteen minutes later. It was a dream start that would raise expectations all round. Slowly but surely, with Greaves' help, West Ham managed to pull themselves out of the relegation zone, beating Liverpool 1–0 at home, Wolves 3–0 and drawing 2–2 at Upton Park with the eventual League runners-up, Leeds.

The Hammers had managed to stay up, finishing in seventeenth place, but a good last furlong could not disguise the fact that they had been well behind the pace all season. It was apparent that Ron Greenwood would have to do some deep thinking during the summer if West Ham were to improve on the results of the 1969/70 season. Meanwhile, Greaves' thoughts turned to the World Cup Rally.

Three months later, after his gruelling excursion to Mexico, Greaves turned his attentions back to his new club and the opening fixtures of the 1970/71 season. The first match was one to whet the appetite of football fans across the country: West Ham v. Spurs at White Hart Lane in front of a crowd of 53,640. The game ended 2–2, and of course Greavsie got on the scoresheet, but despite the fact that he'd notched one up against his old club and received an excellent reception from the Spurs fans, the game merely served to highlight what a big step down the 30-year-old had taken by moving to east London.

Playing against a Spurs side full of cultured flair players with international experience, it struck Greaves that the standard of football at West Ham was nothing more than a poor relation. At Tottenham he had mixed with the likes of Dave Mackay and Alan Gilzean; he had struck up an excellent playing rapport with Cliff Jones, John White and Danny Blanchflower, thriving on their incisive play and vision. They had brought the best out of him. At West Ham it was a different story.

Though he was loath to admit it, his team-mates at West Ham were of a mediocre standard. There was no one there with the strength of Dave Mackay or the grace of Danny Blanchflower. Greaves himself would be the first to admit that he was past his best at the time, but with good players around him, Greaves knew he could get goals for West Ham; sadly, those players were in the minority. His game was spiralling into decline before his eyes, and it depressed him.

Worse still were the fans. They had marvelled over his debut brace against Manchester City and every game expected him to score the goals that had made him such a revelation during his career. When Greaves was unable to recapture the sort of form he'd shown at his peak, the Upton Park crowd – unfairly, perhaps, but certainly predictably – began to get on his back. It was a strange experience. At every club he had played for (even Milan) he had always enjoyed the support of the fans. He'd always been a crowd favourite. At Upton Park it was a different story. They chose to see him as a player who wasn't trying his hardest, someone who would shirk his responsibilities when the going got tough and wouldn't give his all for the team.

Once again West Ham started the new season badly, failing to pick up a win from their first ten games. Once again they found themselves struggling in the bottom three of the table. The club was desperately trying to pick up points, but Greaves' goals had dried up. The fans were obviously unhappy about this state of affairs. In an attempt to ease his depression, Greaves began to drink more heavily after the morning sessions at the club's Chadwell Heath training ground.

West Ham was a very sociable club and had a number of big drinkers. Among the regulars at Jack Slater's pub opposite the Romford Greyhound Stadium were Bobby Moore, John Cushley, Harry Redknapp, Jimmy Lindsay, John Charles and Frank Lampard. Greaves would later claim that the West Ham drinking school could probably out-booze the old Tottenham crowd of Mackay and co. at White Hart Lane. In fact, so renowned were the West Ham crowd for their antics that some of these post-match session tales have attained legendary status.

On one occasion following a Saturday game, Bobby Moore was dragged out of the pub by his mum. The England and West Ham captain had become involved in a round with his team-mates, forgetting that his wife was waiting for him indoors, dressed up for an evening out on the town. His mother had received several distressed phone calls from Moore's wife and was livid. Disregarding her son's reputation, she stormed down to the bar, much to the amusement of Moore's friends and the assorted regulars, and pulled him out of the pub.

'You can't do this, Mum!' he yelped as he was grabbed by the scruff of the neck. 'I'm the England captain!'

Unfortunately his protestations fell on deaf ears. Mrs Moore dragged her son out on to the street and ordered him home.

Despite this lively atmosphere behind the scenes, Greaves was seriously considering retirement. 'I had always promised myself that once I stopped enjoying the game I'd be out,' he wrote later.

I was not kidding myself. I knew I had lost a yard of speed over the last couple of years and that my game could only deteriorate. The fact that things were not going right for me at West Ham had been at the back of my mind for several months. Even as early as September of that season I had considered packing it in. That was after a shocking defeat by Newcastle [they had been beaten 4–1]. I heard that Ron Greenwood was going to resign and I made up my mind that I would leave with him.

I felt that I owed allegiance to Ron, since he was the man who brought me to West Ham. Anyway, nothing came of it and I decided to do my best for him and the club. But the snap had gone out of my game. My confidence went and I began to sense a mood almost of hostility towards me from the fans. Not that I blamed them. I never really turned it on for them, did I?

Ron Greenwood confided in Moore and Greaves about his desire to retire on the way to New York for an exhibition match against Pele's Santos two days after that September defeat at Newcastle. All three were standing in the upstairs bar of a jumbo jet and both players were shocked. Greaves in particular had a great deal of respect for Greenwood, having played for him at England U23 level. The 4–1 defeat had affected the

West Ham manager badly, but not as much as the drink, as Greaves recalled:

> Mooro and I, plus a business pal of his, Freddie Harrison, were getting stuck into the golden liquid in the bar when Greenwood joined us from downstairs and requested a Coke. It was none of my doing but I must admit to having suppressed a juvenile giggle when I noticed Freddie lacing the Coke with Bacardi. Ron was famous in football for being strictly an after-match sherry man, nothing stronger. During the next hour he must have had another five or six Cokes, all of them doctored by the mischievous Harrison, with Mooro and I egging him on with nudges and winks. It was a diabolical thing to do and I don't think Ron ever forgave Mooro and I for it, although we were only onlookers.
>
> Ron finally realised what was going on, and to his credit he laughed it off. The alcohol made his tongue looser than he would have liked and he confessed he was thinking of resigning. I felt choked in a way because here was a man who had always done his honest, level best for West Ham and had made them a club renowned throughout Europe for the quality of their football. But he had recently lost his way and I had done absolutely nothing to help him get back on the right path. Ron was a kind, caring and Christian man in the truest sense, and he did not deserve the old-pro cynicism that I brought into his life.

Following that Bacardi-fuelled heart-to-heart, Greenwood forgot his desire to resign and soldiered on for the rest of the season, but it was obvious the damage had been done. On the pitch things were still going horribly wrong. On 28 November West Ham were beaten by Coventry, a result that put them deep in a relegation battle. Sitting in the bath, the players had been given an hour-long grilling from Ron Greenwood following their poor performance. The water turned cold around them.

Greaves was getting fed up with all this. He had other commitments in his life with his family and the many businesses he'd set up with his brother-in-law, Tom, and several other associates. The feeling that he didn't need football any more, especially as it was now a hardship rather than a pleasure, grew all the while. By the end of the year, his decision to quit was cemented in his own mind.

The decision was confirmed, if it needed to be, on New Year's Day 1971, when West Ham were beaten 4–0 by Blackpool in the FA Cup. The team simply was not good enough and seemed to have lost whatever sense of collective spirit and understanding they'd had in the past. The press slaughtered Greenwood and his players, but worse was to come. It transpired that Greaves, Moore and Clyde Best had been out on the town, seeing in the New Year, without the knowledge of their manager. A fan had seen them out and about and had reported them the next day, before calling up the national press to inform them of the gossip.

Greenwood was furious. In one go he had been let down publicly by his players and humiliated by their shocking performance against poor First Division opposition (Blackpool finished bottom of the table that year). He came down hard on them, fining and dropping all three players. Moore was also subsequently left out of the next England squad by Alf Ramsey. The situation seemed to have spiralled out of control as the club became wrapped up in the media outcry without giving the players a fair hearing. It was the end as far as Greaves was concerned. He knew he'd made a mistake, but a drink before a game didn't merit the punishment they'd received. There were far worse performances on the pitch at Blackpool that day, and they were from players who hadn't even been drinking the night before.

Match days became a real bind. Feeling betrayed, Greaves could not put his heart into the club. He felt that the effects of that evening out in Blackpool had been exaggerated; he knew their antics had not been responsible for the poor performance the following day. Still, he played for West Ham to the best of his ability, but the drive, the passion, had disappeared. He knew at the end of the season he would be retiring.

Spirits were lifted among the fans and players soon after when Greenwood managed to sign Bryan 'Pop' Robson from Newcastle United for £120,000. The England U23 international was rated as an excellent prospect at the time, and he promptly lifted the team with his work rate, scoring on his debut against Nottingham Forest and inspiring the Hammers to a 2–0 win over Ipswich Town the following week, Greaves scoring both goals. The Forest game was the Hammers' first home win since October 1970. Everton, the reigning League champions, were also turned over, then Robson and Hurst scored the goals in a 2–1 win at Upton Park against Manchester United.

On 8 April 1971, Jimmy Greaves scored his last goal in professional football. It was, of course, a match winner, and the victims were West Bromwich Albion. West Ham were clear of relegation, but Greaves felt he had little to celebrate. He knew his career was over. 'I'd provided little to shout about at West Ham,' he said afterwards. 'And once I'd made my mind up about retiring I just wanted to finish quietly. For me it wasn't a happy occasion, but a necessary one.'

When the season officially ended, the 31-year-old Greaves announced his decision to leave football. It was the end of an era; from now on he wanted to be known as Jimmy Greaves the businessman rather than Jimmy Greaves the footballer as he turned his attention to financial activities outside the game. It was a sad loss for English football, but Greaves knew his limitations. He had always been a proud man and wanted to bow out at the highest level. He knew there were several clubs in the lower leagues who would pay him a good wage to play for them, but it didn't seem right. He would later claim that playing for cash rather than honour and trophies would be like prostituting the talent he had.

The football world felt his decision was premature. 'He quit the game far too early at the age of 31,' said Bill Nicholson. 'Jimmy Greaves stayed less than two seasons with West Ham before he announced his retirement. He was a proud man and when he realised that his gift of being able to score remarkable goals was forsaking him, he quit.'

But while fans and players alike bemoaned the loss of one of England's greats, Greaves himself was about to face a far greater personal tragedy. A life without football would be at the very least a half-empty one, and he soon turned to other pursuits to fill his spare time. Afternoons without training and the camaraderie of a squad get-together were soon being spent alone in the pub.

Jimmy Greaves was about to succumb to alcohol addiction.

16 The Lowest Point

No man need die of thirst between London and Southend!

Jimmy Greaves can actually remember the lowest point of his alcoholism years. It was a cold winter's night in 1977. The time was around three in the morning. The former Chelsea, AC Milan, Spurs and West Ham player had spent the last six and a half years away from professional football either in the pub or drinking at home. And the drinking had been heavy and excessive. His wife Irene had expressed her concern on several occasions about his increased alcohol intake, but her warnings had fallen on deaf ears. That winter, Greaves stooped to a new low.

Despite the biting cold and the time of night, Greaves was rooting frantically through his bins in a desperate search for an empty bottle of vodka. Irene had discovered a secret stash of booze in a cabinet as her husband slept in an armchair in the front room following his regular visit to the pub at lunchtime. Angry at her husband's desire to hide the drink from her (owing to the fact, common to all married alcoholics, that she would criticise him for spending the whole of his time drinking rather than with her and their family), Irene decided to do the only thing she could think of. She poured the contents of the bottles down the sink.

She knew her husband would be angry, but Irene had become desperate. Greaves had undergone a dramatic change since he'd retired from top-flight football and she could see no way of helping him. Pleas to stop the drinking often resulted in huge arguments. Sometimes his tantrums would turn nasty, and he'd become angry and violent. He'd smashed up the house before in a drunken rage after a high-volume exchange of words, and naturally Irene was frightened of what might happen if she confronted him again.

Greaves woke up in the dark. The afternoon's session had once again taken its toll and his mouth was dry with the dehydrating after-effects of the booze. The only cure for that thirst was to have another drink. Irene had gone to bed and he knew he could sneak a drink from his secret stash without her knowing anything about it. He had taken to tricking her regularly when it came to taking a drink. She would always complain that he drank too much and would nag him whenever he had a glass in his hand, so to ease the tension and disguise the amount of alcohol he had been taking during the day, Greaves would drain his glass whenever her back was turned and refill it before she had the chance to see what he'd done.

And by this stage Greaves had taken to consuming a frightening amount of alcohol on a daily basis. His life was one big destructive routine. The morning would start the same way, every day: Greaves would awake hung over and shaking. Like any alcoholic, he'd convinced himself that the only way to shake the fug off, achieve any sense of clarity and get rid of the shakes and twitches was to take another drink. He would regularly knock back half a bottle of vodka before he had even stepped out of bed. When he'd actually managed to get dressed, he'd roll out of the house and down to the local pub.

A brisk walk from house to bar gave him the chance to compose himself – he didn't want whoever was serving him to see he was struggling with the shakes, that he was already half cut. By opening time, Greaves would be at the front door of the local boozer, waiting for the landlord to open up and pour him his first pint of the day. He always ordered a pint of Guinness first as it was the nearest thing he could get to breakfast; after that he'd drink a further seven or eight pints with several shots of vodka. At 2.30 in the afternoon, when in those days the pubs had to turn their customers out, Greaves would usually just go straight home to sleep in his armchair.

With that first session of the day slept off by the early evening, Greaves would leave the house again, to arrive as the pubs reopened. He'd sink another seven or eight pints and would often return home at closing time to drain one, sometimes two more bottles of vodka before bedtime.

It was a horrific amount of alcohol for anyone to take day after day, but Greaves was comfortable enough financially to afford large quantities of good-quality drink. He knew that if he hadn't had the luxury of being able to afford top-quality alcohol and was relying on a cheaper form of spirit, he would probably be a dead man by now. Like any alcoholic, the quantity of booze he was consuming didn't seem to have an affect on him physically. Sure, he'd piled on a few stone since retiring from the game, but most people put that down to an understandable reduction in the amount of exercise he was taking. Certainly no one ever assumed that Greaves had become an alcoholic. He had the ability to disguise his blurred state of mind with a calm assurance and never looked as though he had consumed a skinful.

Standing by the cabinet, Greaves was confused. He had hunted high and low looking for his bottles of drink, in the places where he remembered hiding them from Irene before, and found nothing. Tipping the house upside down to see if she had hidden them somewhere else, Greaves was struck by the awful truth: she had thrown his booze away. Frantically stepping out of the house and rummaging through the bins outside, Greaves came across several empty bottles. To most people it would have been enough to accept that there would be no more drinking until the next day, but to the alcoholic, there might have been one or two last drops of booze left. Pulling out the bottles one by one, Greaves desperately shook them, draining the last drips of vodka in an attempt to get one last drink. It was a tragic situation. One of football's greatest entertainers was now hopelessly ill and in danger of spiralling out of control. He needed help.

Sadly, the stories about Greaves' drinking have tended to overshadow his phenomenal football career. Like George Best, a player who suffered similar problems at the same time, Greaves will be remembered as a drinker by those who aren't old enough to have witnessed his skill and grace on the football pitch. A player who went off the rails and succumbed to the boredom that comes with a life away from the game with nothing to do rather than spend the long days in the pub, bookmaker's or living room.

It seems too simple to dismiss Greaves' drinking as a product of boredom and frustration at not being able to perform every Saturday afternoon, but his hopeless addiction was certainly linked to the nature of professional football. Players tend to have a lot of time on their hands when away from the game. Training usually finishes around one o'clock, and by the time the players have had lunch and a rubdown, the afternoons are free to spend at home or out on the golf course. For modern-day players, this 'time off' allows them to fulfil media commitments and corporate responsibilities, to prepare mentally and physically for any forthcoming game. Players are amply warned about the dangers of having too much free time and are actively discouraged from taking alcohol. For players plying their trade in Greaves' era, however, life away from football was a completely different proposition.

Players were actively encouraged to drink together after a match as it was deemed part of the team bonding process. An afternoon in the pub together was seen as the perfect way to unwind after a difficult game and ideal to build a strong sense of team spirit within the club. Most players saw drinking after a game or training as a perfect release from the boredom and the pressure that came with playing in front of thousands of people every weekend and the increasing media attention and high-profile nature of the sport. The management at most clubs would often turn a blind eye to alcohol intake by squad members as long as it didn't affect their performances on a Saturday afternoon. As long as the players worked hard in training and performed well on the park every week, what harm could a few drinks cause? The truth was that alcohol was doing them very little good; most managers and coaches were unaware of the extent of alcohol consumption in their ranks.

The football culture in Britain has always been based on drinking. Before any game, whether it's a Premiership fixture or a tie between two Third Division sides, the local pubs in the vicinity of the ground are packed with fans eagerly discussing the forthcoming match, and they refill again at five o'clock for the post-match analysis. Before the introduction of Continental players and coaches, football players had a similar attitude: the team would disappear to the pub after a bath to conduct a post mortem of the game. It was a wonder that more players weren't struck down with the disease of alcoholism.

Former Portsmouth striker Mickey Quinn gave his explanation of the old football attitude to drinking between games: 'I used to enjoy myself, but I'd always be in for training. And don't get me wrong, I trained hard. It seemed that as long as you were at the training ground on time and capable of running a few laps around the pitches, there wasn't a problem.' Arsenal bad boy Peter Storey had a similar attitude: 'From the time I first kicked a ball as a pro, I began to learn what the game was all about. It's about drunken parties that go on for days. The orgies, the birds and all the fabulous money. Football is just a distraction, but you're so fit you can carry on with all the high living in secret and still play the game.'

The problem seems to be disappearing from the game now, but there have been one or two high-profile victims in recent years, most notably Tony Adams and Paul Merson, both of whom admitted to their alcohol addictions in the 1990s. Adams himself shone a light on why footballers are so susceptible to succumbing to alcohol during their careers when he admitted he would drink to relieve the immense pressure he felt before a game. England matches were particularly bad: 'I needed a drink before I joined up with England, because I was so full of fear.' It's a feeling shared by thousands of other footballers of every grade every week.

Adams hit rock bottom after a depressing Euro 96. The highs of beating Scotland in the group stages of the tournament and reaching the semi-finals were quickly overshadowed by the low of losing to Germany in the semis on penalty kicks. The Arsenal captain proceeded to go on an eight-week bender, drinking copious amounts of alcohol to ease the sadness he was feeling. His marriage was in tatters and he was suffering from excruciating pain due to an injury to his knee.

Like Greaves, Adams can remember the lowest point of his illness when he awoke from a drunken slumber in a hotel room, surrounded by the contents of his mini bar and lying next to a woman. Adams had no idea who she was, what her name was or how he had met her. This experience, combined with a 58-day spell in Chelmsford prison following a drink-driving conviction, encouraged Adams to turn to Alcoholics Anonymous for help. He experienced a dramatic and encouraging recovery, moving away from his dependence on drink to rejuvenate his career. Afternoons in the pub were replaced by afternoons spent reading literature, watching theatre or staying at home learning to play the piano. Adams emerged from the fug of alcoholism a stronger person, skippering Arsenal to a second historic Double in 1998. Football had superseded alcohol as the emotional crutch in his life, but for Jimmy Greaves there was no such support.

His life had developed a dangerous routine, but footballers, like soldiers, are creatures of routine. Training starts at 9.30 and finishes at 12.30 every day. During that time everything is regimented. Away trips are organised to a tight schedule, and each player is informed of the moment when they should get on the team coach. Players have to wear set tracksuits at certain times. They have to eat together at the same time. Go to bed at the same time. Get up at the same time. Warm up at the same time. Leave the ground at the same time once the game is over.

When their careers are over, psychologically they are wired to develop a lifestyle based on routine, and there's nothing wrong with that, provided the day-to-day routine is a healthy one. It's once the player slips into bad habits that the problems arise, when the euphoric highs when the team claims a victory and the depressing lows suffered when the team loses become difficult to cope with. For many players, the best way to calm the adrenalin rush of winning in front of a packed house of 40,000 people is to drink. Losers experience a similar desire.

Jimmy Greaves finds it difficult to pinpoint the exact moment the drinking became compulsive, but he acknowledges that the death of his son Jimmy Junior in 1961 and the stressful move to Milan were big factors. 'Within weeks of our losing our darling Jimmy, I was pitched into a traumatic transfer drama that had so many twists and turns that it was a wonder I stayed sane. It involved a move to Italy and into a world in which I found I needed to drink to help blot out the nightmare I was living. I spent four months in Milan. It seemed like a lifetime. I was a kid when I went out there and felt like an old man by the time Spurs received me.' It was undoubtedly a depressing time for the Londoner as he experienced a crippling loss of freedom and an overwhelming sense of homesickness, combined with the pain of bereavement. It would have been enough to send the strongest of people into a decline. It was this dangerous cocktail of emotions that initially forced Greaves to turn to the bottle. The fact that he had few friends in the city and even fewer who could speak the same language meant he was a very lonely individual and would drink in the evenings to ease the boredom.

Greaves would often sneak away from the attentions of his oppressive coach Nero Rocco to get a cheeky beer and drown his sorrows. Until that point, Greaves had always been a social drinker; now it had become a necessity. At Chelsea he always had a drink after the game, but he was never a heavy boozer. There was nothing he liked more than socialising after a game, but that was purely because of the love of the company rather than a taste for the beer. After a match he would always be in the local pub with the rest of the team reliving every kick of the match with his friends over a beer or two. At that stage of his career Greaves was something of a lightweight in drinking terms and could only handle a few beers, but this was largely down to the fact that he wasn't earning the big money he would later pick up at Milan and Spurs and couldn't afford to drink heavily. Footballers in the 1950s had very little disposable income, and much of Greaves' money was going on the essentials in life. He was only earning £17 a week during the season and £8 a week when the football programme was over; most of this cash went on Irene and their modest flat in Wimbledon. There was very little extra to spend. Most of Greaves' team-mates were big drinkers, but at this stage in his career he would drink in order to temper the adrenalin rush of playing professional football rather than to slay the demons of deep-rooted psychological problems.

Milan, however, was the beginning of the end for Greaves. The drinking quickly became the only way to live his life in any form of comfort as the transfer debate between Chelsea and Milan spiralled out of control. 'Those were the days when I started visiting pubs as a regular habit, a hobby even, rather than as an after-thought,' Greaves wrote in *This One's On Me*, an autobiography dedicated to his drinking problem.

> When I was standing at a bar with a pint of beer in my hand it was as if the problem of the Milan affair would shrink to manageable proportions. Even now, you ask me how to get to any place on the east side of the Aldgate Pump out into deepest Essex and I will direct you by pub names. You want to get to Southend from London? From Mooro's – the pub run by my old drinking partner Bobby Moore at Stratford – come up past the Two Puddings on to the A11, past The Charleston, The Thatched House, The Bell and The Red Lion before taking the A12 at the Green Man, Leytonstone. Follow the road down past the George, Wanstead, The Redhouse, Redbridge, Oscars, Newbury Park, and after you have passed The Moby Dick at Chadwell Heath take the flyover at Gallows Corner on to the A127. From here it's a straight run to Southend passing the Fairlane Motel, The Halfway House, The Brighton Run, The Fortune of War and finally The Weir at Rayleigh!

The Milan-bound player was positively well oiled whenever possible. For his journey out to Milan for his debut against Botafogo in the San Siro, Greaves missed his scheduled flight because he had been drinking champagne with a journalist from the *Daily Express*. By the time they had booked another flight (to a completely different airport 30 miles away from Milan), Greaves had had a skinful, his fear of flying exacerbating the problem. Later, of course, Bill Nicholson would allow Greaves and Cliff Jones a few drinks because of this; one can't imagine Arsène Wenger allowing Dennis Bergkamp the same luxury today. So Greaves was drunk before he had even stepped on to Italian soil. That didn't bode too well for the future.

Greaves drank for the next four months, but still at this stage it wasn't yet an addiction; certainly the drinking wasn't as excessive as reported in the Italian national press, who tagged Greaves as a drunken, womanising animal. The move back home, to Spurs, provided some much-needed relief and the drinking returned to being an important but more controlled social element of Greaves' life, never a necessity. Tottenham Hotspur was the location for Jimmy Greaves' golden years as a player, and it was here that drinking once again became an enjoyable experience. The players were determined to mingle after games and a large number of them would be in the pub almost immediately after the match had finished and the communal bath drained away. It didn't take long for Greaves to be accepted by Spurs, both on and off the pitch. He scored a hat-trick on his debut at White Hart Lane and was soon accepted off the pitch by his peers, joining Dave Mackay and Bill Brown, among others, in the Bell and Hare or the White Hart – two pubs near the ground – for drinks after every home match.

Both manager Bill Nicholson and Eddie Bailey were aware of the drinking going on after the games, but weren't sure of the extent of the players' consumption. They certainly would have been shocked had they seen the amount of beer put away by their team every Saturday afternoon in N17, a fact that's clear from Nicholson's reflections on the matter:

After a match Jimmy enjoyed a lager. Late on in his career I know Jimmy opened a pub for a friend of his and that might have been the start of his drinking heavily. I had no idea what he was drinking. I know Alan Gilzean was a drinker. He liked Bacardi and Coke. There were a few players who didn't drink at all. Most of them took a lager. There is a lot of free time in football and a lot of energy expended. It is normal to drink and I let them get on with it as it was done in moderation and didn't affect their performances ... I was amazed some years later to hear of his [Greaves'] revelations about drink and how he became an alcoholic. I must say he never gave me reason to suspect that he had a problem. It certainly never interfered with his football, or lessened his professionalism.

Spurs more often than not found their games tough, especially in the 1961/62 season. They were the League champions and FA Cup holders and everyone wanted to beat them. For the opposition the visit of Spurs or a trip to White Hart Lane was the equivalent of a cup final. As a result, the players would find their games emotionally and physically draining and Greaves and his team-mates would work up a thirst every Saturday afternoon. Every pub session was instigated by Dave Mackay. The Scotsman was as hard a drinker as he was a player and would often be found propping up the bar, buying the drinks and holding court about the team's performance that afternoon. Only Danny Blanchflower didn't drink.

The players felt that a good drinking session wouldn't do them any harm. Greaves and his colleagues would never leave after one or two pints and would often consume a large amount of beer before moving on to the stronger spirits for the rest of the evening. They could sweat all the booze out with a run the following day if they wanted to. Anyway, they were fit enough to need only a day's recovery from a big session and wouldn't be affected when training came around again on the Monday. None of them was aware of the damage they were doing to their bodies; the afternoons spent in the pub unwinding after the game were as natural and essential as the day-to-day training regime imposed by Nicholson and Bailey.

Even when the Spurs Double-winning team began to break up in the mid 1960s, the drinking culture at the club remained. Joe Kinnear, Alan Gilzean and Phil Beal replaced Mackay, John White and Bill Brown as Greaves' drinking partners, and others around Greaves began to notice he was drinking to excess, even though to look at him when he was in the pub you would never have thought he was drunk. He had the ability to disguise the fact by sitting quietly, puffing on a pipe, giving off an air of control, of someone who had only taken in one or two pints. The reality was far different.

Nicholson first became particularly concerned for the player after the European Cup Winners' Cup tie in 1967 against Hadjuk Split in Yugoslavia. Following an encouraging victory over the Yugoslavians, Nicholson took his players to a nightclub to help them let off steam, as a reward for an excellent performance. It wasn't the sort of behaviour encouraged by the Spurs manager, but a few journalists had been into town the night before and had been taken by a 'cabaret' act that involved a busty woman performing tricks with a rope and a tiger skin. The team went together and enjoyed a good drink, Greaves in particular leading the way. He'd taken in ten pints when some locals encouraged him to try a particularly lethal local spirit called slivovich. Ten shots later Greaves was several sheets to the wind.

Deciding it would be unwise to approach Greaves that evening, so poor a state was he in, Nicholson took the striker to one side on the plane home and gave him a friendly warning. In Nicholson's mind it was a kindly way of curbing any problems that might develop later on should Greaves continue binging. Little did he know that the damage had already been done, that the England international was already on a slippery slope to alcoholism.

17 The Slippery Slope

Once I had five, six or seven lagers in me I would get a click in my head and the world would seem a rosy place.

JIMMY GREAVES, 1979

Even the responsibility of playing for England didn't dissuade Jimmy Greaves from drinking. In fact, the prestige of playing for his country was often excuse enough to meet up with old pals and hit a few bars in a foreign country. It was a sociable atmosphere on England duty, but there were limits. While Greaves and his friends were looking for places to go and bars in which to drink, their manager Alf Ramsey was keeping a strict eye on his players and would not tolerate any misbehaviour. Ramsey was a hard manager who liked to keep discipline, and woe betide anyone he caught drinking without his permission. Greaves and Ramsey crossed paths on several occasions over the issue, but it didn't stop the striker from trying his best to get away from the England camp while on foreign soil to sample the local liquor.

Ramsey knew his players liked to drink and knew which players in particular were fonder of the booze than others. He was loath to tolerate any nonsense, but he knew there would be no harm in allowing his players a beer or two after a match providing they all drank together and he was in their midst. There was no point in using beer as a team-building tool if half the team was absent from the bar. It was important that all were in attendance and that the drinking was kept to a minimum.

Always at the bar alongside Greaves at England get-togethers would be Bobby Moore. Greaves would later admit he thought the England captain had 'hollow legs', such was his ability to hold huge amounts of booze. He also claimed the West Ham player was 'untouchable' in a drinking contest. Moore and Greaves loved to unwind together after a game, and like Greaves, the drink would never show on Moore's face. No matter how much alcohol he had inside him, his face always remained calm, giving the impression he was as sober as a judge when in reality he was bordering on the legless. Moore wasn't, however, an alcoholic.

Together they incurred the wrath of Ramsey on more than one occasion, and both trod a fine line between enjoying some harmless fun and risking serious disciplinary action at the hands of the FA. On one occasion, in May 1964, both were nearly sent home along with several other respected internationals after a night out on the town in London's West End. The squad was due to fly out to Lisbon the following day to play a friendly against Portugal, but Greaves and co. saw no harm in sneaking out of the team hotel for a few drinks to unwind before the big game. Among the group were Bobby Charlton, Gordon Banks and Ray Wilson, all later to become World Cup winners. None of them returned to the hotel before midnight. Alf Ramsey had noticed their absence that evening and was not going to let their crime go unpunished. When the players returned to their rooms they found their passports (which had been left for safekeeping with the coaching staff) laid out on their beds. It was a chilling reminder that any further misdemeanours would not be tolerated.

Nothing was said to the players for four days, giving the impression that Ramsey had either forgotten about the incident, such was his concern about the Portugal fixture, or they'd managed to get away with it because the England manager was in one of his more lenient moods. Nothing could have been further from the truth. Following Ramsey's last team meeting on the evening before the game, the manager made a worrying request. Sending the team away to bed, he asked to see the seven players 'who I believe would like to stay behind and see me'. Greaves had miscalculated Ramsey's mood and attitude. He was angry, in no mood to ignore misbehaviour from his players.

'You are all very lucky to be here,' he announced to his visibly nervous players. 'If there had been enough players in the squad, I would have left you behind in London. All I hope is that you have learnt your lesson and will not do anything silly again.'

All seven players featured in the Portugal game, which England won 4–3, with the England goals coming from Charlton and John 'Budgie' Byrne, who scored a hat-trick. Both players had been involved in that notorious drinking session. It seemed that Ramsey's psychological reprimand had worked on the pitch, but it was to prove useless off it.

Ten days later England were scheduled to play the United States in New York. Once again, Greaves and Moore were the culprits, sneaking out of the hotel to see Ella Fitzgerald in concert. Both players were massive fans of Fitzgerald and had been rested for the game against the USA the following night. There seemed no harm in leaving the hotel for a few hours to watch a concert and take in a few bars. It wasn't as if they had a game to worry about the next day, and if the manager didn't know, there wouldn't really be a problem. But Ramsey made it his business to know the activities of every single one of his players and was aware of the movements of both Greaves and Moore. The following morning when the players gathered for breakfast, Ramsey ignored them. He wasn't in the mood to reprimand them there and then, but he wanted them to know that their actions had been noted and would not be forgotten.

But if Greaves and Moore were troublemakers while on England duty, they were positively lawless when turning out for West Ham. Greaves was at a low point in his career at this stage. He had just been released by

Spurs, the club to which he had given his best years, and the move, although it had seemed like a good idea at the time, had broken his heart. He'd also left the England set-up in a less than perfect way. Once again he was turning to drink for support through this difficult period, and it was perhaps inevitable that worse was to come. If the drinking had been heavy at Spurs with Mackay, Gilzean et al, then Greaves was about to discover a new meaning to the term 'Quick one for the road?'

Upton Park had its fair share of drinkers when Greaves arrived in the spring of 1970. Bobby Moore, Frank Lampard and Harry Redknapp were all regular boozers after the match, discussing the afternoon's performance – and there was always plenty to talk about. West Ham were not a stylish unit and were firmly parked at the wrong end of the First Division table. The football was poor, totally unlike the slick, crisp passing employed by Spurs to dominate games. Greaves was struggling to adjust to the new style, and the poor results and performances began to depress him. The only answer seemed to be to drown his sorrows after every game and blot out the memory of another shocking personal performance.

He was never short of company. Saturday afternoons would be spent with the same faces in the same pubs, conducting another post mortem on the afternoon's game. And by now the drinking was causing a problem on the pitch as well as off it, such were the amounts Greaves was consuming. In a successful Spurs side, Greaves could handle the odd poor game if the team had won, which they invariably had. At West Ham, where results didn't come so easily and the side had to work much harder as a result, Greaves found the going tough and struggled to come up with match-winning performances.

Things came to a head after the media scandal at Blackpool in the FA Cup on New Year's Day 1971. Greaves had already had a miserable start to the season and had nearly quit the club, along with his manager Ron Greenwood, as early as September that year following a 4–1 thrashing at the hands of Newcastle. 'The Blackpool Affair', as it was nicknamed by the national press, was to prove the final straw as several West Ham players, Greaves among them, were harshly criticised for a blatant lack of professionalism.

West Ham had travelled up the coast for the tie against Blackpool on New Year's Eve. Having to travel away from your family on a national holiday is bad enough, but having to worry about an early night and an important FA Cup fixture the following morning when everybody else is partying is enough to send anyone round the twist.

Mooro and I were preparing to go to bed after a couple of lagers each in the restaurant of the Imperial Hotel where West Ham were staying on the eve of the FA Cup tie against Blackpool. As we were walking through the hotel lobby we got into conversation with some BBC television cameramen who were in town to film our match. They were waiting for a taxi to take them to ex-boxer Brian London's 007 nightclub. 'There's little chance of the game being played tomorrow,' one of the cameramen said. 'The pitch is iced over. It will be a miracle if it's fit for play. I think we're all wasting our time up here. What a way to start a New Year.'

A doorman then called out to the chatting group, informing them that two taxis had arrived to take them into town. The cameramen looked confused. They had only ordered one, but Greaves reacted quickly. If the game was going to be called off tomorrow, there would be no harm in taking the other taxi into town and having a few drinks to see the New Year in. Bobby Moore, agreeing it was a good idea, grabbed two other West Ham players – Clyde Best and Brian Dear – from the bar and dragged them along. London greeted them at his nightclub door and invited them in for drinks. Moore and Dear knocked back five pints with Best sticking to the soft drinks. Greaves, meanwhile, proceeded to polish off nearly twelve beers. By a quarter to two in the morning all four players were back in the hotel restaurant ordering sandwiches and coffee, blissfully unaware that the Blackpool pitch was about to be passed fit for play the following morning.

It was a disgraceful decision. The pitch had been solid with frost and was slippery underfoot, but worse than the state of the pitch for West Ham was the result: the Hammers lost heavily to a poor Blackpool team, Bobby Moore in particular struggling to play anywhere near his best. The team was criticised for the result the following morning, and by Monday night they were public targets. A fan had made a phone call to the club and a newspaper saying he had seen Greaves, Moore, Best and Dear drunk in Brian London's nightclub on the eve of the match. All hell broke loose. The press had a field day, most papers featuring the fiasco on the front pages. The scandal dragged on for weeks, Moore suffering most of all from the bad publicity. He was the England captain; he'd lifted the World Cup just four and a half years earlier and was big-name news; it was only natural that the papers should take an exaggerated interest in his activities. And the negative headlines were to have a far-reaching effect. Moore was dropped from the England squad for the European Championship qualifying fixture against Malta the following month as a result of the incident in Blackpool.

Greaves was at his wits' end. The bad publicity and poor results on the pitch meant he was becoming frustrated and depressed. The drink was now a necessity, and Greaves was in the throes of the first stages of alcoholism. 'In my last few months at West Ham I began to shift beer in bigger quantities than ever,' he wrote after retiring from football. 'After training at Chadwell Heath I would go to Jack Slater's pub opposite Romford Greyhound Stadium and drink right through until closing time. Most evenings I would prop up a number of bars near my Upminster home. Suddenly football didn't matter to me any more. All I was interested in was drinking.'

When he announced his retirement, Greaves consigned himself to a perilous life away from football. Ideally it would have meant spending the rest of his life concentrating on the packaging business he had built up with his brother-in-law, but it was going to be spent concentrating on drinking heavily. The business the pair of them had built up was a successful one. Started with a £1,000 bank loan taken out on his return from Milan, the business slowly began to build itself up, churning out cardboard boxes. When Greaves retired the company had subsidiaries in a country club, a transport firm, several sports shops, a few travel agencies and a ladies'-wear shop. All that promise of a secure and happy future was to be treated with neglect.

At first Greaves did pay a daily visit to the offices, if only for a couple of hours before he could make his way to the nearest pub once it had opened for business. Later he would take the office to the pub, where, as chairman of the company, he would entertain clients and propose business ventures. By 1973 the interest in the business had waned completely; Greaves was only interested in spending whatever profits he made on drink.

His judgement was shot to pieces by the booze, and he made error after financial error. At home, things became even worse as he took to continual drinking, day after day. Gone were the days when drink had appealed because it meant the sociable atmosphere of a packed pub where he could stand alongside his friends and laugh about the day's events. No such camaraderie now; Greaves found drinking at home far more appealing. Irene was shocked at the state of her husband. She could not bear to see the man she loved reduce himself to a drunken wreck and pleaded with him to take a good, hard look at himself, but it was no good. Greaves was too far gone. 'I found there was no way I could go a waking hour without a drink,' he admitted later. 'I started to smuggle bottles of vodka into the house and hide them out of Irene's sight so she didn't know just how much I was getting down me.'

At the supermarket he was equally crafty, buying a bag of fruit to disguise the fact that the only reason he had travelled to the shop was to buy more booze. Of course Greaves knew he was an alcoholic at this stage, but he could do nothing about it. Between them, Greaves and his wife decided that maybe a return to football might be a cure for his drinking problem. It was obvious the alcohol intake had increased once he'd decided to quit football, so maybe a return to the game was the answer. Greaves grasped at the straw and made a return with Brentwood and later Chelmsford, but it was a futile effort. He was not fit enough and the football was of a poor standard, depressing him even more. It meant a swift return to the bottle.

More worrying than the amount of drink Greaves was consuming were the risks he was taking. On several occasions he drove home after consuming nearly twenty pints of beer and several shorts. He was once woken up at the side of a road by a policeman after he had fallen asleep at the wheel of his car and swerved across to the other side. He told the officer he had merely pulled over to get some sleep and was going to drive once he felt a little bit more refreshed. The policeman believed his excuse, advising him to keep the windows wound down if he felt tired. And the risks impinged on his family too. At home, Irene was becoming increasingly worried by Greaves' violent mood swings and encouraged him to visit a private nursing clinic where his problems could be dealt with professionally.

In the meantime, Greaves took to appearing in charity golf matches, five-a-side games and squash matches. To the public, he appeared a normal person. Nobody had any idea of the raging emotional timebomb that was ticking inside. Such was his fitness and ability to turn on the style when he played that the then Spurs manager, Keith Burkinshaw, and Bill Nicholson actually discussed the possibility of a comeback following an impressive performance in Pat Jennings' testimonial at White Hart Lane. Greaves declined, not because the move didn't appeal to him, but because he knew he could not be trusted and didn't want to let down the club he had loved most of all.

The clinic initially had some success as well. After several weeks of treatment, Greaves' lust for drink was reduced, and for two months after the sessions were over he was able to go without a drink. With his cravings apparently banished for ever, Greaves foolishly reverted to drinking just one or two pints a day. Of course, the one or two pints soon turned into four or five, and before long he was back to the old daily routine of throwing as much down his neck as he possibly could. As a result, for about another year Greaves' life followed a depressing pattern:

He would hit the booze.

On Irene's insistence he would go back to the clinic.

He would leave the clinic 'cured'.

After a month or so, he'd be back on the booze again.

Irene had had enough. So had her brother Tom, who found he could do little but watch the business disappear in smoke owing to his partner's reluctance to leave the pub and join him in the office. Tom, moreover, was becoming increasingly angry at the emotional strain Greaves was putting his sister under, and after some persuasion Greaves sold out his share of the business.

Psychiatrists continued to come and go in a vain attempt to help Greaves, but to no avail, and in the winter of 1977 he was taken to an alcoholic ward in a mental hospital in Chelmsford, Essex. The doctors informed him he was going to kill himself if he carried on at his present rate, again with little effect. Greaves, terrified he would become a permanent resident as he looked at the patients around him, decided to discharge himself the next night.

Three weeks later he was hospitalised again, this time in a mental hospital in Warley. Worse was to come: the tabloid newspapers had got hold of the story and the lurid details of Greaves' demise was soon public knowledge. Irene could take no more and asked him to leave. Greaves moved back to his parents' house, leaving Irene alone in the house with the four children. Irene also managed to win the rights to Greaves' business interests and sold them, enabling her to buy the house they had built up together. But Greaves wasn't bitter about the situation. He knew he'd got himself into this mess, that there was no one else to blame.

There was no way our marriage could survive the pressures that I put on it. I can remember little of it, but I am assured that during my worst drinking bouts I was a pig of a man. I can recall the nightmares of the DTs, lying on my back shaking uncontrollably and having all sorts of terrifying hallucinations. Walls moved and came crashing towards me, inanimate objects became mobile, horrific figures, and I could see haunting faces in every corner of the room. I was in hell.

I would stumble around the house with a three-day growth of stubble on my chin, not knowing whether it was night or day. I could no longer afford the luxury of private nursing homes. When I became impossible to handle, friends used to take me to the alcoholic ward of Warley mental hospital. I was there so many times they must have thought I was a member of the staff.

The only place left to turn to was Alcoholics Anonymous. It was to prove a wise move. By visiting the AA, Greaves learnt how to live his life again without the aid of drink. It was a difficult period in his life in which he had to face up to the awful mistakes he had made in the sober light of day. He is now the first to admit that his years spent at the bottom of a pint glass are nothing but a distant memory. In fact, he has a limited memory when it comes to his playing career, such was his intake of alcohol at various stages of his life. In an attempt to avoid visiting the pub as he dried himself out, Greaves would shut himself away in his one-bedroom flat and watch films to kill the long days without drink. Evenings out would be spent with his friends from the AA, avoiding the lure of pubs and bars at all costs.

He also made a return to football with Barnet Football Club. Many of Greaves' associates felt he would fall apart at any given moment and that the reformed alcoholic was still a ticking timebomb waiting to go off again. They were to be proved wrong. Greaves continued to play football for Barnet as he battled against the booze, repaying chairman Dave Under-wood's faith in him with some sterling performances in the Southern League. He had pulled his life together, in spite of all the hardships he had experienced over the past ten years.

And at the time of his signing there was some interest from other clubs, most notably San Antonio FC from the NASL in America. A representative of the club got in touch with Greaves and asked if the player was interested in a move across the pond. Greaves declined – America, he decided, was too far to go – but the official would surely have had second thoughts had he seen where his transfer target was conducting the telephone meeting from: Greaves was flat on his back in a hospital bed in Warley mental hospital, shaking with the DT's and struggling to hold the phone in his hand.

With his problems now seemingly behind him and his darker years public knowledge, Greaves found himself in a position to carry on living his life once more. Sure, he had to take stick from the occasional idiot on the street, or the odd nasty chant from the away fans at Barnet, but it was nothing more than he could handle. After what he had endured over the past ten years, a cry of 'Don't hit the bar, Greavsie!' wasn't going to upset him.

He was sober again, and doing what he loved doing best: playing football.

18 The Road to Recovery

At Barnet, we really saw what Jimmy Greaves was all about. Sure he was past his best, but at that level he was different class.

LES EASON, BARNET TEAM-MATE, 2000

It was a brave admission from someone who had been in the public eye for so long, especially when Greaves knew it was likely, as in fact later happened, that he'd become the daily centre of attention in the tabloid press as they relived every gory detail of his fall from grace. While the regular meetings with the AA were helping him through this depressing and traumatic drying-out process, Greaves needed another emotional crutch to help him through. Drink was his support when the football wasn't going well; now that he had turned full circle, it was the turn of football to play that crucial role.

Greaves had been playing the occasional game for non-League side Chelmsford City and appearing in the odd charity match to pass away the time in between drinking sessions, but now, in an attempt to banish the alcohol once and for all, he turned his attention back to football and his business interests full time. Barnet chairman Dave Underwood was working with Greaves at the time with a fund-raising organisation called The Gold Diggers. The group would raise money for charity by organising fun matches with former professionals and pro-celebrity golf days, and included Jimmy Hill and Eric Morecambe among their numbers. Realising that Greaves was looking to play a more regular and disciplined form of football than he was used to at

Chelmsford City, Underwood asked him to turn out for Barnet.

Greaves jumped at the chance. The Bees had just been promoted to the Southern League Premiership and were playing an attractive form of football. Manager Billy Meadows had rebuilt the side that had been relegated two seasons previously and employed a bunch of former professionals to take his club back into the top League. His plan had worked, the likes of Terry Mancini (ex-Arsenal) and Bob McNab (ex-Wolves) helping him gain promotion immediately, but that wasn't enough for the club. The Conference was in the process of being formed at that time, and to qualify, clubs in the Southern Premier League would have to stay in the top half of the table for ten years as the Northern and Southern Premier League formed an alliance. With Greaves in the side, that ambition could be realised. Still, his signing came as a shock to both fans and players alike. 'We couldn't believe it,' recalled striker Les Eason, who played for Barnet for ten years between 1968 and 1978.

I used to go to watch him at White Hart Lane in the 1960s during the Glory years and he was a hero of mine. I used to love watching Greavsie, because I was a striker and he was so good at scoring goals it was unbelievable. He was one of the best strikers in the world at the time, if not the best, and suddenly he was playing for us. There were all these rumours flying around in the local press and the club that he was signing for us, but nobody wanted to get their hopes up, but then he turned up at training. We were gobsmacked. I couldn't believe it. All of a sudden I'm in the same team as one of my idols. It was a little strange to say the least.

Greaves settled in quite quickly and made his debut in August 1977 in the opening game of the season, against Atherstone Town at Barnet's home ground, Underhill.

It was going to be a memorable game for all the wrong reasons, as for the first time in his career Jimmy Greaves failed to score in a debut game, despite the fact that Barnet won 3–2. Fortunately the Bees' faithful didn't have to wait long to see Greaves hit the back of the net: in a 2–2 draw away to Worcester City on 3 September, he scored his first goal in a Barnet shirt, doubling his tally a week later in a home fixture against Minehead. The win in that game was a significant one. Minehead had finished second in the League the previous season behind Wimbledon and were a respected outfit; the result signified Barnet's ability to compete with the top teams in the League, despite the fact that they had been promoted only the previous season.

Greaves scored the winning goal, but the game proved to be a bit of a culture shock for a player used to scoring in the lofty heights of the First Division and Serie A. Wheeling away in delight, Greaves turned to run towards the crowd, only to be reminded that there was no crowd! A modest gate of 886 had turned up to watch Barnet play that weekend and they were dispersed around the ground. The best Greaves could manage was a handful of home fans, so he ran towards them with his arms raised in triumph. It was a far cry from the thousands that had shared in his celebrations when he'd scored at White Hart Lane or Wembley. His team-mates sympathised, as Eason recalled:

I think it took him a little while to get used to the style of play and the way of living in the lower leagues. But I think he quite enjoyed it and he was given special allowances to the rest of us because of what he was going through. All the drinking stuff came out around the time he joined the club, but it didn't seem to affect him. He didn't have to go to training because of what was going on around him at the time. But there were so many games in our League at that time that we were playing three or four times a week and so you didn't really have to train to keep sharp. There was no need for somebody like him to train because he was 38, and when you're that age, the training can be a bit too much. It was important he got through the games and so we let him off.

We played him up front at first, but he was such a good all-round player that we dropped him back in midfield, so he could have a more influential role in the game. Sometimes we would drop him just behind the front two and the team was geared around him. But even though he was playing in the middle of the park, he still scored 25 goals. The man was so good at running off the ball and receiving passes, you could see 'why he was such a good player in the First Division. We played him in midfield because he didn't have the legs to run around up front and chase a lot of lost-cause passes, but he also had a good footballing brain and he was still very mobile. You wouldn't have thought his body had gone through all the punishment he had put it through with all the drinking. He was in great shape, he was very nimble and he survived on his brain rather than his speed.

On the ball it was apparent he was a better player than the rest of us. His tactics were superb, and when you play with non-League players, they spend a lot of the time without the ball because they're not good enough to keep hold of it, especially when the games are a bit rough and tumble. Greavsie would have the ball all the time. He was always one step ahead of the rest of us, which was good for us and bad as well, because he would play a pass that a Cliff Jones or John White would have got on to in the Spurs team, but someone of our standard wouldn't expect it.

The fans took to Greaves immediately and appreciated his experience and cultured touch. Strangely, his arrival at Underhill didn't result in a massive increase in gates, although the crowds were usually larger than they had been – partly because, sadly for Greaves and Barnet, his off-the-field behaviour was the subject of a lot of interest from the national press, who would travel to Barnet matches with the intention of studying the recovering alcoholic. Sometimes the battle against alcohol would become too much and Greaves wouldn't even show up at the ground on a Saturday afternoon when the club had a home fixture. 'It was strange, because he wouldn't turn up for the odd game and no one would talk about it,' remembered Eason.

The manager, Bill, said we should just get used to it. We didn't know what he was on about because the drinking wasn't public knowledge at that time, but when it did come out, it just clicked. I never thought it was anything to do with the drink, but that was a natural reaction, I suppose. I didn't want to think bad of the bloke, especially as I respected him so much. When it did come out in the papers it was all a bit of a shock, but looking back it should have been obvious. His daughter used to drive him to the ground before all the games; we didn't realise it at the time, but it was because he had been drinking. There was one game where he turned up late and he had just come from wherever he had been drinking. He dropped out of the team that day and it was put down to a bout of flu. Nobody wanted to believe any different.

I think Billy and the chairman knew about it. He must have done because he was the manager, but it never came out in the club until the papers got the story out halfway through the season. I'm sure there were people at the club who did know, but nobody said anything to anyone. The chairman would have known, and I think he would have been looking after him financially. Whether any other player would have been allowed to turn up late or miss games is doubtful, but you had to make exceptions. He was Jimmy Greaves, after all.

The drink never affected him physically. Put it this way, we never saw him drink when he was at the club and he didn't look like he was on the booze. I've seen a lot more players who were supposed to be in good condition playing with more weight than Jim had. Take the John Hartsons of this world. They can struggle with the weight sometimes, but at 38 Greavsie still looked fit and was in good condition. He was still mobile, which was important to us.

In his first season with the club, 1977/78, Greaves scored 25 goals and finished up as Player of the Year. Barnet finished seventh in the League. But in the close season there was more turmoil at Underhill: Billy Meadows decided he'd had enough of football management and quit the club. Barry Fry was drafted in as his replacement. Fry was manager at Dunstable Town and had been approached by the club before Meadows' appointment. He had turned the job down at the time, but felt the move up to the Southern Premier League two years later was an ideal one. But while the move was an excellent step for his career, he found that Meadows had left one or two problems behind. Having been made up of retired pros, the average age of the Barnet team was around 37. Meadows had drafted in a lot of experienced players for short-term success, but it meant most of them were past their best, even for non-League level. Fry started the clear-out as soon as he took up his new post, but Greaves was still in his plans.

Greaves, meanwhile, was enjoying his time at the club, and his new-found role in midfield appealed to him. 'Barnet are a great little club,' he wrote at the time.

And I am more than thankful to them for continuing to have faith in me, despite my problems. I am enjoying my football more than ever before in my life. It is a release valve from all the tensions and pressures, the opposite of when I used to be a First Division footballer. In those days it was a cause of many of my problems and I turned to drink as a crutch. Now I am leaning heavily on football to help me through my crisis.

Now I'm happy playing a midfield role for Barnet, spraying passes around, Rivelino style. I leave the goalscoring to others. I did my fair share of that in the First Division. There has been a marvellous private and public reaction to my confessions of being an alcoholic. I've had hundreds of letters of support, sympathy and understanding from close friends and also from strangers who I have never met but identify with me through football.

Barry Fry was equally impressed with his efforts at the club and continued to play him in the middle of the park, despite his desperation to build a younger side.

Whenever he played he was brilliant. At one end he would be kicking the ball off our goal line and at the other he would be banging them in. He was fantastic. I know it's a cliché, but he would cover every blade of grass over 90 minutes. He certainly didn't waltz around the pitch like a prima donna, and of course the fans and the players loved him for it. He was great for the team and great for the club. The weird thing was, he was coming off the booze at the time and he was on top form. You wouldn't have guessed he had a drink problem, because he looked as fit as anyone on the park.

It was very difficult for him and for the club, because his drink problem was in the papers quite a lot. There was a lot of attention on him, but it didn't seem to bother him at all. You could tell he enjoyed his football, in fact I think it helped him through it all. He wasn't one of those retired professionals who went into the lower leagues to pick up a pay cheque and not put any effort into the game. He tried as hard for us as he did in the First Division. He wasn't going to pick his money up and ponce around. He wanted to win for Barnet and we loved him for it.

He was 38, but he was so fit. He used to get back and help in defence and he would take all the corners and throw-ins and free kicks. He was totally involved in the game and he had a brilliant attitude. The players respected him, and none of them were in awe of him or anything like that. He was one of the lads. They all got on really well with him, but that was Jim's personality. He was easy to get on with and he was always a good laugh and a great person to have in the dressing room. The club was very supportive towards him as well, but to be fair he got through it all on his own. On and off the pitch he was a credit to Barnet Football Club.

However, Greaves did disgrace himself once with an uncharacteristic outburst on the pitch during a first-round FA Cup tie. The London club had qualified from the preliminary stages for the first round proper for the second year on the trot, a new experience for Greaves:

I remember pre-season training at Barnet and being told that we were playing Camberley Town on the Saturday. I asked why this was and I was told that it was an FA Cup match. Normally my involvement in the FA Cup would begin in January, but we were playing in a preliminary round and that season we played about five games in all before we got through to the first round, and I can safely say that I'm one of the very few players to have played in every round of the FA Cup.

In the first round that year they were drawn against the Surrey side Woking. After fifteen minutes, Barnet earned a free kick just outside the Woking penalty area. In an inspired flash of brilliance, Greaves fired the ball around the wall that was still organising itself, past the keeper and into the back of the net. Thinking he had scored, Greaves took the congratulations of his team-mates, only to see the referee re-spotting the ball outside the Woking penalty area. He had disallowed the free kick for being taken too quickly! Greaves was furious and began remonstrating with the official. As the argument became more and more heated Greaves became more and more aggressive until the referee was left with no option. Greaves was off.

Despite his absence, Barnet went on to secure a replay with a 3–3 draw, but their midfielder would be forced to sit on the bench for the second game through suspension. Another 3–3 draw followed, before Woking claimed a 3–0 victory in the third game.

Only months into the 1978/79 season, though, it was becoming obvious that Greaves could not carry on giving his full attention to the club. His business commitments outside the club and his battle against alcohol meant he was becoming increasingly absent from games and training. Following a brief meeting with Barry Fry in January 1979, Greaves felt it was in the interests of both the club and himself if he left. Fry recalled:

Jimmy decided to leave because of everything that was going on around him. He had a lot of pressure off the pitch, what with his business commitments and his personal life, and he couldn't give us his full time. He felt it would be better to leave than to let us down. I was very disappointed because he was a great ambassador for Barnet and it was a real shame to see him go. He was still a great player, so he was a loss on the pitch. We did everything we could for him and would let him off training, because we knew he would keep himself fit and he never let us down on a Saturday afternoon. But it wasn't enough for him, so he left.

Greaves has fond memories of the time he spent at Underhill with the Bees:

I had an enjoyable time at Barnet . . . I played some great games with the club. I thoroughly enjoyed it. It was a refreshing change because for my entire career I had been in top-flight football and my time at Barnet was an experience I will never forget. For example, we would often board a dodgy coach to go to away games and we'd stop off at a motorway café to have a pre-match meal of sausage, eggs and chips. I remember on one occasion we were heading off to Bath City for a match and the coach actually broke down. We eventually arrived 45 minutes late and the referee gave us ten minutes to get changed and get out on to the pitch. It was a 0–0 draw, so the fans weren't too pleased with us that day.

The atmosphere at Barnet was great, and even though we didn't have many supporters, it was always a pleasure to turn out for Barnet. I had the pleasure of turning out alongside Steve Oliver, Terry Tappin and Johnny Fairbrother, and the Southern League was a good standard of football. During my time at Barnet I played in midfield and was nominated as captain. I had relinquished my goal-scoring responsibilities and turned into a clogger! Dennis Brown, who was a striker, relinquished the captaincy and gave me the honour, although I must add that I never asked for it. The average age of the side was fairly old, so when I went up for the toss before kick-off I would always make sure that we kicked up the hill in the first half . . . purely because we were all so old that we didn't have the strength to play up it in the second.

Barnet had a great reputation and that's why I signed for them. During my time with them I saw parts of the world I had never seen before, for example towns like Nuneaton, Grantham and Weymouth. I had a wonderful time.

If Barnet left an impression on Greaves, his time at the club certainly left an impression on the team, its players and the supporters. For a brief moment, the club was the centre of attention as all the focus of the sports media turned its attention towards Underhill. Les Eason, for one, reckoned Greaves was great for the club. 'I suppose it's like Michael Owen going to Bromley FC or somewhere like that. He scored 25 goals a season from midfield and there was so much to his game. He scored three or four wonderful free kicks and his passing was great. He was the best goalscorer in the world in his time, and I think he would have been an even better player if he had been playing today.'

Epilogue

He'll always be remembered as one of the greats, despite his laid-back attitude off the pitch.

ALAN MULLERY, 2000

It's hard to look back at Jimmy Greaves' career and not feel a pang of regret. Certainly when one considers an overview of the striker's career one can only ask the question 'What if?' Sure, Greaves enjoyed some wonderful highs during his time at Chelsea and Spurs and scored a phenomenal amount of goals in an England shirt, but we can only debate how short of the line he was in terms of being one of the world's greatest ever strikers. What if he hadn't moved to AC Milan? What if he hadn't been struck down by hepatitis in the lead-up to the 1966 World Cup and played in the nation's biggest ever game? What if he hadn't hit the booze during the low points in his life? What if he hadn't moved to Upton Park? And what if he hadn't retired at such an early age?

Certainly, every player has to endure a certain amount of regret and ask whether his career would have taken a different course had he made a different decision somewhere along the line. Greaves experienced so many crossroads, however, had so many hurdles to cross, that it's hard not to wonder how his life would have turned out had he enjoyed a degree of good fortune at those vital junctions in his life. One can only wonder at what Greaves makes of it all. A place in a World Cup-winning side would top his wish list for sure, as would a few more years in the colours of his beloved Spurs. But one thing's for certain: had he not become an alcoholic his life would have taken a very different course. Surprisingly, the alcohol is not his biggest regret.

> The biggest regret of my whole football career was leaving White Hart Lane in 1970. Bill Nicholson swapped me for Martin Peters and off I went to West Ham. It was a mistake, and I think Bill would admit it now too. I should have sat tight, stayed put and proved that even if Peters came I was still going to be the main man. But at the time I thought, 'If that's the way you want it, then I'll go.' I will still always have an affection for West Ham but, in truth, I lost something inside with that move. My interest in football weakened after that. I was heartbroken.

It's a sad truth that Greaves remembers very little of his career, owing to the fact that his memory has been fogged by the booze. Indeed, it is so clouded that he finds it difficult to recall what onlookers remember as the great moments in his life. 'It's amazing how many times I get asked to name my greatest goal. People can't understand when I struggle to give them a quick answer. I honestly meant it when I gave the stock answer that every goal is great if it goes in the back of the net. They all had a certain merit. Goals were my business. It wasn't a larkabout. There was something special hearing the swish of a ball hitting the back of the net.'

But maybe the fact that he has trouble recalling long periods of his career is a blessing in disguise, considering the heartbreak and frustration he experienced at certain times in his life. More than anything, it is a credit to his character that he managed to fight back against a crippling illness and play for Barnet FC. It was a strength that would later see him resurrect his career alongside Ian St John as a popular TV pundit and football columnist for the *Sun*.

Alan Mullery, for one, wasn't surprised that Jim made something of himself after his career was finished.

Sure the Spurs deal broke his heart, but after all the trouble he went through, he bounced back. Bill knew what he was doing when he sold Jim, but a lot of people started to criticise Bill. Still, he made the right decision. Jimmy wasn't the same at West Ham and Martin was a wonderful player for us, so you can't really criticise Bill for it. But it was a shame to see him go. I think that started the change in him. Bill saw he was never going to be the player he was in previous years and I think that happens to us all, doesn't it? We get to a stage where we can't do the things we used to do easily and that's what happened to Jim. It's the manager's choice.

He always had his fingers in other pies. He went to a rally during the World Cup in 1970 and I think Bill might have taken that as a sign he wasn't totally interested in football any more. But he was always involved in other things was Jimmy. He always wanted to do other things outside football and he was one of the first footballers I knew with a business interest outside the game. In fact, he was the one who was always reading the *Financial Times* on the train or in the club canteen.

He was an entertainer. He was a great goalscorer, a wonderful character and a pleasure to have worked with. He made football look easy, even when he wasn't playing well, and he loved to be involved in the game. Being away from football caused him problems because he adored the game so much and lived for it. Leaving it behind broke his heart.

Jim played football for fun. It was always a game to him. But unlike other players, he was an absolute genius at it. That's the thing.

Jimmy Greaves Factfile

Born: 20 February 1940, East Ham

League goals

CHELSEA

1957/58	22 goals	
1958/59	32 goals	Div One top scorer
1959/60	29 goals	
1960/61	41 goals	Div One top scorer

TOTTENHAM HOTSPUR

1961/62	21 goals	
1962/63	37 goals	Div One top scorer
1963/64	35 goals	Div One top scorer
1964/65	29 goals	Div One top scorer
1965/66	15 goals	
1966/67	25 goals	
1967/68	23 goals	
1968/69	27 goals	Div One top scorer

TOTTENHAM HOTSPUR/WEST HAM

1969/70	12 goals
1970/71	9 goals

Total   357 goals

Serie A goals

AC MILAN
1961/62   9 goals

England goals
57 caps – 44 goals

May 1959	Peru	L 1–4	1 goal
May 1959	Mexico	L 1–2	
May 1959	USA	W 8–1	
October 1959	Wales	D 1–1	1 goal
October 1959	Sweden	L 2–3	
May 1960	Yugoslavia	D 3–3	1 goal

May 1960	Spain	L 0–3	
October 1960	N. Ireland	W 5–2	2 goals
October 1960	Luxembourg	W 9–0	3 goals
October 1960	Spain	W 4–2	1 goal
November 1960	Wales	W 5–1	2 goals
April 1961	Scotland	W 9–3	3 goals
May 1961	Portugal	D 1–1	
May 1961	Italy	W 3–2	1 goal
May 1961	Austria	L 1–3	1 goal
April 1962	Scotland	L 0–2	
May 1962	Switzerland	W 3–1	
May 1962	Peru	W 4–0	3 goals
May 1962	Hungary	L 1–2	
June 1962	Argentina	W 3–1	1 goal
June 1962	Bulgaria	D 0–0	
June 1962	Brazil	L 1–3	
October 1962	France	D 1–1	
October 1962	N. Ireland	W 3–1	1 goal
November 1962	Wales	W 4–0	1 goal
February 1963	France	L 2–5	
April 1963	Scotland	L 1–2	
May 1963	Brazil	D 1–1	
May 1963	Czechoslovakia	W 4–2	2 goals
June 1963	Switzerland	W 8–1	
October 1963	Wales	W 4–0	1 goal
October 1963	Rest of World	W 2–1	1 goal
November 1963	N. Ireland	W 8–3	4 goals
May 1964	Uruguay	W 2–1	
May 1964	Portugal	W 4–3	
May 1964	Rep. of Ireland	W 3–1	1 goal
May 1964	Brazil	L 1–5	1 goal
June 1964	Portugal	D 1–1	
June 1964	Argentina	L 0–1	
October 1964	N. Ireland	W 4–3	3 goals
October 1964	Belgium	D 2–2	
December 1964	Holland	D 1–1	1 goal
April 1965	Scotland	D 2–2	1 goal
May 1965	Hungary	W 1–0	1 goal
May 1965	Yugoslavia	D 1–1	

October 1965	Wales	D 0–0	
October 1965	Austria	L 2–3	
May 1966	Yugoslavia	W 2–0	1 goal
June 1966	Norway	W 6–1	4 goals
July 1966	Denmark	W 2–0	
July 1966	Poland	W 1–0	
July 1966	Uruguay	D 0–0	
July 1966	Mexico	W 2–0	
July 1966	France	W 2–0	
April 1967	Scotland	L 2–3	
May 1967	Spain	W 2–0	1 goal
May 1967	Austria	W 1–0	

Bibliography

Books

Barrett, Norman, *The Daily Telegraph Football Chronicle* (Colour Library Direct, 1993)

Betts, Graham, *Spurs: Day-to-Day Life at White Hart Lane* (Mainstream Publishing, 1998)

Bowler, Dave, *Danny Blanchflower – A Biography of a Visionary* (Victor Gollancz, 1997)

Butler, Bryon, *100 Seasons of League Football* (Queen Anne Press, 1998)

Clarke, Brian, *Docherty* (The Kingswood Press, 1991)

The Complete Guide to England Players Since 1945 (Stanley Paul, 1993)

Davies, Hunter, *Glory Game* (Mainstream Publishing, 1972)

—— *Joe Kinnear: Still Crazy* (Andre Deutsch, 2000)

The Essential History Of West Ham United (Headline, 2000)

Ferris, Ken, *The Double* (Two Heads Publishing, 1996)

Fry, Barry, *Big Fry: The Autobiography* (Collins Willow, 2000)

Greaves, Jimmy, *This One's On Me* (Readers Union, 1979)

Greaves, Jimmy and Gutteridge, Reg, *Let's Be Honest* (Pelham Books, 1972)

Haynes, Johnny, *It's All in the Game* (The Sportsman's Book Club, 1963)

Hill, Jimmy, Greaves, Jimmy and Kaye, Nicholas, *A Funny Thing Happened On My Way to Spurs* (1962)

Holmes, Bob (ed), *My Greatest Game* (Mainstream Publishing, 1993)

Hughman, Barry J. (ed), *The PFA Premier and Football League Players' Records 1946–1998* (Queen Anne Press, 1998)

Hurst, Geoff, *The World Game* (The Sportsman's Book Club, 1968)

The Jimmy Hill Story (Hodder & Stoughton, 1998)

Leatherdale, Clive, *West Ham United – From Greenwood to Redknapp* (Desert Island Books, 1998)

Mackay, Dave, *Soccer My Spur* (The Soccer Book Club, 1961)

Miller, David, *The Boys Of '66* (Pavilion, 1986)

—— *Cup Magic* (Sidgwick & Jackson, 1981)

Moore, Brian, *The Final Score* (Coronet, 2000)

Nicholson, Bill, *Glory, Glory: My Life With Spurs* (Macmillan, 1984)

Northcutt, John and Shoesmith, Roy, *West Ham United: An Illustrated History* (Breedon Books, 1997)

Ramsey, Alf, *The England Years* (Chameleon Books, 1998)

Venables, Terry and Hanson, Neil, *Venables: The Autobiography* (Michael Joseph, 1994)

Wolstenholme, Kenneth, *They Think It's All Over* (Robson Books, 1998)

Newspapers and magazines

FourFourTwo
Daily Telegraph
Daily Mail
Express
Sun
Star
London Evening News
Guardian
The Times
Observer
Daily Mirror
Daily Herald

Index